You've Got a Hair Out Of Place!

Let me FIX the Whole in Your Head.

JAMIE GILLETTE PARKER, LOIS LOYEK

BALBOA.PRESS

A DIVISION OF HAY HOUSE

Balboa Press books may be ordered through booksellers or by contacting:

Balboa Press
A Division of Hay House
1663 Liberty Drive
Bloomington, IN 47403
www.balboapress.com
844-682-1282

Because of the dynamic nature of the Internet, any web addresses or links contained in this book may have changed since publication and may no longer be valid. The views expressed in this work are solely those of the author and do not necessarily reflect the views of the publisher, and the publisher hereby disclaims any responsibility for them.

The author of this book does not dispense medical advice or prescribe the use of any technique as a form of treatment for physical, emotional, or medical problems without the advice of a physician, either directly or indirectly. The intent of the author is only to offer information of a general nature to help you in your quest for emotional and spiritual well-being. In the event you use any of the information in this book for yourself, which is your constitutional right, the author and the publisher assume no responsibility for your actions.

Any people depicted in stock imagery provided by Getty Images are models, and such images are being used for illustrative purposes only.
Certain stock imagery © Getty Images.

Print information available on the last page.

ISBN: 978-1-9822-6445-1 (sc)
ISBN: 978-1-9822-6447-5 (hc)
ISBN: 978-1-9822-6446-8 (e)

Library of Congress Control Number: 2021903427

Balboa Press rev. date: 02/22/2021

Disclaimer

As authors of "You've Got a Hair Out of Place" we wish you to recognize that All Characters and their stories, names, and location are false, merely created as examples to convey Inspiring Ideas and Techniques we have used in our own lives to find comfort.

They do not at all resemble real people.

Naming the BOOK

For your greater understanding of the Title given this Book.

It was August, yes. We were about to move far away. The Move was a surprise and sudden shift in direction for us. Downsize was in order. "Big Yard Sale".

My Mother found out we were moving and having this Sale indirectly. We had not had time to inform her, considering a place was bought and the former place sold in less than 3 days. We hardly had time for the business at hand let alone inform family and friends.

To make a long story short, it had upset her deeply. She rallied the 'troops' and had the whole gang at the Sale *'lest we sell the family heirlooms'* which we had bought back from her auction 2 years earlier. Her own guilt had set in, not ours as our children claimed those unique pieces already.

Since Mom and all her surviving children were in one place, a sister with a new Photographic Interest decided we required a Family Photo.

Mom was well sprayed and elegant. I on the other hand, was into the return to a more natural hair style. Besides, I had been up for more than 12 hours – out in the breeze and sunshine.

She took her place at the end of the veranda poised and pretty. As I walked toward her, she said **"You've Got a hair out of place."**

I said with a bit of disdain in my voice *"Which one"* did she not understanding hair was the last thing on my To Do list this day?

Two years later, in a shopping mall a flight away from home, 2 ladies were in front of me in Spokane, ID. As we walked out, of the washroom, they were flipping a curl of the one who just came from the Hairdresser.

I remarked "that reminds me of the Book I am writing."

"Oh!" they say. "What is the name of the Book?"

"You've Got a Hair Out Of Place". As they laughed and told me it was one, they wanted to read and added the Subline *"Let Me FIX that Whole in Your Head".*

"WHY FIX WHAT IS
ALREADY WHOLE?"

What if our *'Hair out of place'* is the **Talent**,
the **Gift** we have to offer the World in LOVE?

The Gift that fulfills,
PEACE IN EARTH.

One day we simply Decide to STOP
Marching in Someone else's Parade.

We simply Decide to return to Child Curiosity
& Observation, to Joyfully Engage the
Splendour of LOVE's **Integrity InnerNet**
EVERY MOMENT.

We Decide to Embrace Beauty & Peace:
To Joyfully Frolic –
Light in Our Own Integrity

Praise for the Book

"I've only had opportunity to finish reading up to Chapter 7 in this book. However, I am already enchanted with the characters introduced and find the unique way the author has intertwined fiction and life coaching knowledge with personal experiences very intriguing. I look forward to the next chapter in the journey."

T. F.
Human Service Worker
Adult Survivor of Childhood Sexual Abuse

I have learned our wellbeing manifests our choice of focus. It is revealed in our attitude, thoughts, words, actions, and comportment.

L.L.
Retired Minister

The Authors told us to read from front to back for the best conclusion. I am glad I did, for the final paragraph totally blew me away. **Save the end of the book for the end** and you will be amazed at the Wisdom offered through their amazing Story Telling abilities.

L.Y.
Author and Designer
And yes, a Survivor

I just finished reading your book. Wow! From first sentence you grabbed my curiosity. Mind bending, twisty-turns, thought provoking are a few words that come to mind. Enjoy the Journey.

Sylvia
C.I.D.E.S.C.O.

Honoring

The Memory of our Beloved Mothers!

Unexpectedly, they gave Title to this Book.

My Mother Being the Entertainer &
Excellent Hostess that she was, she would
love knowing she was 'Famous' for this.

We highly respect the lessons they taught through
their own pain and emotional entanglement.

Dedicated

To our Coaches

To our Mentors

To our Soulmates

Dedicated to our Clients that encouraged us to keep writing because they <u>Required a New Story for themselves</u>.

The Real-Life Stories of moving Beyond Generational, Parental, Governmental, Religious and Social Beliefs that poison and imprison in an Emotional Dungeon.

The Story of moving beyond sexual abuse and many other traumatic experiences.

A New Story beyond – Honoring the
Integrity of our own InnerNet.

Dear Friends, here we are with the New Story Created out of your experiences and ours.

Warning

This may not be for innocent ears. There are references to sexual misbehavior. No, the few examples I use are not the worst I have heard in my Coaching Career.

And yet, the Point Must Be Made for the Rights of Women. These are not rare cases. These are stories happening in Ordinary Homes and Families in your Neighbourhood.

It is TIME to Wake Up and Speak Up.

It is TIME to pay Attention to them.
These FROZEN VOICES.

These are your daughters and grandchildren.

These are your wives and girl friends.

LISTEN! Allow their Voices to Be HEARD.

However, you have been warned. There are accounts of sexual violence in a couple of chapters. The milder experiences of a lot of my clients.

Apologies in Advance

Our apologies for any reason you feel like we have misrepresented your country, citizens, behavior, or any other irritation. This is deliberately Written in Novel Form to avoid offences.

If an event is different than you remember it being, then remember this is how it occurred to me in my memory bank. Rather than become offended because you believe I misrepresented you or the event, then WRITE YOUR OWN BOOK the way you remember it being.

The Only Truth is LOVE.

Whatever you believe as being the Truth of an event is simply your <u>Perception</u>. Whatever I believe as being the Truth of an event, is simply my <u>Perception</u>. A third party would have an even different Perception than either of us.

If the Perception this book takes irritates you, then maybe you have issues that require searching and gaining the victory over. They may be undermining your wellness and causing Emotional Stress as well.

Thank you!

Preface

Have you left your Birth Country as a child?

Have you entered a New School System, vastly different than you know?

Have you grown up with Overwhelmed/Overworked Parents?
(*and their secrets*)

Have you ever felt like the Ugly Duckling – the Stranger in your Family?

Have you experienced sexual abuse as a child? A teen? A woman?

Have you ever been shipped off to University to take the Education '*Expected of you*' but not your choice; an education that did not Honour YOUR TALENTS?

Have you ever been a Stranger in a Strange Land? found yourself 'with child' = PREGNANT, scared, traumatize by attitudes around you?

Have you ever returned Home to find your parents wanted nothing to do with "*The Stain*" you put upon their *seeming Immaculate Reputation* – to find all your things were already moved to a remote location – isolated?

Have you ever suffered depression and medication overload?

Have you ever been a Single Parent?

I have! My name is Jamie Gillette Parker

This is my RISE.

Unexpected Compulsion

Life is full of writing. I write a lot.

Life Purpose (Lois Loyek)
Desire to be a Published Author since 5th grade.

My Coaching is all about Empowering Emotional Flexibility to move above presenting issues and into the <u>Magnitude of Possibility</u> to LOVE their Incredible.

We cannot Correct an issue from the
same Energy it was Created.

Move up!

By September 2020, after having a Spotlight in a Women's Show, I decided the Book I had been writing was for My Own Learning and Growth. I took *Book Publishing off* my 'To Do List' even though I had paid good money for a Publishing Package more than a year before. I decided maybe I just needed to accept my age and settle into Retirement.

I was TIRED. Sort of!

I was 73.

7 Days later, September 27, 2020 I was given the Vision/Dream of the Characters and the 1st Chapters as I was awakened in the morning. ***This was no longer 'just for my healing'.***

This is the BOOK

This is the format and story that required writing – unfolding as sure as anything. Inspired, I look forward to Writing Sessions, just as you do to the suspense of the next chapter.

It is Curiosity not Will Power
in the Driver's Seat NOW.

I have no idea until it is on the page and I read it as you are. To be honest, I have no idea what will flow or how. Will it be another Page or another Painting Inserted?

I know it will be beyond me to work in all the Coaching.
– The LOVE of who we are Created to BE - The Greatness of the InnerNet etc.

In the end, I feel like this Book is just as my Paintings are:

– I simply Hold the Brush!

I am a Conduit through which the Spirit has chosen to Connect YOU to YOUR OWN Integrity InnerNet.

To show you how you can disconnect from the intensity of the Internet, media, Social Media etc. Disconnect from the FEAR placed upon a plandemic time in history.

A Scamdemic spreading the Virus of <u>FEAR and Imply</u>.

Foreword

Received from a Client in appreciation of a Coaching Session. When I received this email, I had forgotten that this was a process I used with Clients when I first started Coaching many years ago.

It is a powerful restructuring of the Energy Field within us. Enjoy her message of her healing from what took place with her. We appreciate your sharing this with us dear Sylvia.

To the Readers of "You've Got a Hair Out of Place"

As I sank into the rocking chair, emotionally exhausted from the day. My Sister lovingly applied essential oils to my feet. There were tears of exasperation as my potential retreated into a guarded place within.

She quietly listened to my sporadic thoughts verbalized now & then thru sobs and tears. Handing me the rose oil; she asked me to breathe its essence.

She continued to gently stroke an array of oils onto my feet and calves. Exchanging the Rose for Melissa I breathed the essence of the oil in… the tears abated, and I closed my eyes.

Her voice gentle and confident began to guide me on a journey within that involved all my little beings of Protection – the filters of protection I had adopted as I grew up. "All my little girls" she called them.

She led me to the wildflower meadow surrounded by evergreens and birch. The tall grasses caressing my calves where eventually I danced and skipped as a child. Alas, I lay down in the soft grasses and flowers. My tactile senses relished in the cool warmth of the vegetation, that seemed to swallow me into their enchanted place they called home.

Arising, I walked to the other side of the meadow down a small slope where the path narrowed through lush green trees and roses leading to a sandy strip by the tinkling brook. I lay down there…Awe!

Breath-by-breath, letting go of the cares and burdens I had carried there. Inhaling…exhaling…heartbeat by heartbeat I let them go. Until I too was the sand, the water, the sun, and the air. As I looked down, from above in my minds eye I only seen my impression in the sand where I once lay. I had become the Love molecules that had buoyed me up. There I stayed for some time basking in God's gentle all encompassing Love and Comfort.

At some point my attention was drawn once again to the impression in the damp sands where slowly my body manifested. First my feet perfect and glowing. Then the beautifully defined calves and legs; strong. Gently flowing into my pelvis and hips; healthy and feminine. The core of my body, exquisite with perfect functioning organs framed by spine & ribs all in their place. Revealing healthy rounded breasts and shoulders. The silky skin accented a beautiful neck and head with a sound mind and shining ash colored hair. There I lay, my skinny jeans rolled to my calves, my nautical white and sky-blue striped tee, sleeves gently covering my elbows. I slipped back in.

Slowly sitting, I stretched and arched lifting my hands towards God. I was happy to be a live. I got up and found as I stepped upon the brook,

I was on top of the crystal water. That was delightful. As I crossed the brook stepping from stone to stone, I was filled with life abundantly.

Ascending the mountain on the other side I was accompanied by all my little girls dressed in summer dresses busily chattering amongst themselves scampering here and there through the mossy enchanted forest floor. My constant companions, I loved them so.

Upon reaching the mountain top, appeared a Great being Majestic… Loving… Kind. He welcomed us and told us how pleased he was that we had come. In awe we basked in his presence safe soothing healing. He asked the little ones to join him a little way off. He praised them for being my faithful companions and for the fine work they had done.

As they respectfully sat at his feet wide eyed in wonder, he told them of a new plan and one by one instructed them of their tasks ahead. They became excited of the prospect of their new details. All smiling broadly they quietly returned to my side; such immense loyalty they had for me.

The Great One took me into his arms and as he gently hugged me, I was filled with a renewed essence of life. He thanked me for bringing him my burdens and cares. And in that moment, he imparted to me a glimpse of my full potential and allowed me to see all the love I had surrounding me and all the encouragers cheering me on. He bid me adieu and slowly returned to a realm I could no longer see.

Silently in joy, I and the little girls made our way down the mountain, across the brook and entered the wildflower meadow once again.

I lingered back in deep reflection while the girls went on ahead putting their plans together. As I walked through the tall grasses and wildflowers; the aroma filling the air, I was in me, yet I was watching me from on high. Walking in deep thought appreciating my healthy beautiful being. My hair glistened by the sun's rays. My tanned forearm wore three delicate golden bangles, my decollate was adorned with a golden thread that held a small diamond and on my hand a ring. I felt the love that surrounded me. And I felt the love deep within. I could perceive love emanating from me. I understood now that I had a purpose. The purpose to give hope to others!

I saw myself sitting on a rock in a garden holding the hand of an elderly woman showing her hope. I could see me walking with a young mom lifting her spirits believing in her allowing her to believe in herself. I saw me embrace an elderly man as he wept reassuring him of his value. Yes, this is who I really am. Yes, it truly is about love towards my fellow kin who also take their journey upon this plane.

As I reached the other side of the meadow and stepped forward onto the gravel parkway where my girls all gathered in delight. I realized them presenting me with this little red sports car. When only yesterday I thought the SUV would be a practical choice. I slipped into the contoured leather seat and slowly drove away heading towards my cabin in the woods.

As I write this the sound of a harp gently permeates the air, I know this is what I must do, "Give hope to others".

Thank you, God, for fans along the way like Sisters.

Introduction

I awaken early morning. Is this a Dream - I am still asleep?
Is this a Vision I am being given?

We have been working on the details of a Book for an awfully long time. The Title has never changed. We have written a lot. We have no particular order that forms a book.

Procrastination is always an easy choice.

I have been told often that I will expose someone who does not want exposure if I write a Self-help book; or a book based on my life and Coaching experience.

I am confused and wonder if I even need to write this Book?

Who am I writing it for? Why do I feel so compelled to write and yet not have a form in which the reader can understand? Or even a Tribe, a specific reader group I am writing too?

Then September 27, 2020 VISION

I see the main Characters.

I see the first screen and the look on the faces.

I know I MUST WRITE AND PUBLISH.

And still, I wonder "Who is my Audience, my Reader?"

I am told I cannot write to everybody. I must choose my Tribe – my Reader.

'WHO?' I still have no idea.

(Well, actually I do know who, but this is not something I wanted to write about. I wanted to write about something more Inspiring. Yet, more than half my clients have experienced sexual misuse.

First, it was up to me to let go of any Personal Agenda and write what I was given to write. In the end, I cannot say I wrote this. I am so grateful to have gotten to know Jamie so well and have her assistance in all of this. She taught me so much more in four months.)

However, just as I glimpsed the 2020 VISION of the main Characters, I know that We are <u>being Guided</u> in the writing of this Book, just as I (Jamie) was guided into the things I read and devoured as a Teen; just as I was in choosing Lifestyle Designer Coach as a Career. As I Paint, releasing the Tension of the Past. We teach our Clients 'Ponder Painting' as well.

The 'fear of failure OR is it the '*fear of Success*'? - that is still a panic within all of us. And maybe your chief fear as well.

And here we are, together, between the Covers of this Novel. A Story we can relate to, is always a Seller, will always find a common audience. We are as curious as to how this unfolds as YOU are, Dear Reader!

At this point, we have no idea what is coming next, just as you.

The difference?
You hold a completed Book.
We are still writing.

You, *if you wish to dull the excitement*, could go to the last chapter, and see how it ends.

We CAN NOT – for the LAST CHAPTER has not yet been given to write.

Therefore, with common Childlike Curiosity, let us discover together what it is about Living LOVE (Capitalized LOVE) we all Require KNOWING.

Please remember that you will know more about the 'family dynamics' and characters than they know about each other. What they know about each other, is extremely limited as in most family dynamics.

You, Dear Reader, have the advantage as you read the chapters of each one's life. They can only guess how the other thinks, or even who they are.

These people are Family.

These people are Friends and Neighbors.

These people are coaching clients and medical patients.

You will recognize them in your Hometown too.

This is My Story. Our Story.

This is YOUR Story.

This is the Story of being Human in a world of Masked Identities. Hopefully, you will learn to BE Real.

We as humans draw a lot of assumptions. We assume the other knows – BUT only to our own detriment. Ass-U-me and I make an Ass of U and Me.

If you really need to get a complete view of each character, you could go to the chapters that speak about that person. However, you would soon lose interest and miss the suspense.

OR maybe not!

Definitely - you would miss the LOVE Lessons.

This is how life and love unfold. We really do not know the Profile of anyone else. We get glimpses and pieces <u>through whatever lens</u> **WE are looking through** *in the moment*.

Yet as humans, we do a lot of judging from our less than perfect 2020 Vision.

Our suggestion is that you read cover to cover the first time. There are a lot of Life/LOVE Lessons threaded through this Book.

Each Lesson magnifies LOVE.

Welcome - Pleasant Listeners!

This is a LOVE STORY Way Deeper than Human's Love.

AND Yes, this is a Possibility when we give up any Personal Agenda the EGO insists upon.

Surrender to the higher calling and LOVE!

Chapter 1

Jack Williams reached the Property to which he was to size up the structural details, as to whether the building was Structurally worth investing a lot of money into upgrades. It was about 80 feet up on a Beach Front Property, off the beaten trail. He understood it was a recent inheritance.

The woman he talked to wanted to turn it into "a Secluded Spa Bed and Breakfast" – of particular interest to those who were Authoring a Book and required the Quiet she could offer in this relatively isolated location. And maybe adding some of her ideas for a Frolic/Retreat Center to rent and to do classes from.

He had been sent what he was not sure were photos or photos of paintings - of the outside for advanced evaluation. Certainly, there was potential. A rare find on the Island, as it was a large property and relatively undeveloped other than a small building site, which looked rather old and in need of a lot of TLC.

Jack lifted the old brass knocker and rapped it 3 times. A young boy opened the door and peered around the edge of it. His eyes were about the level of the doorknob.

Jack was Silenced by the unexpected!

Am I Dreaming?

Jack felt like he was looking into his own younger face again. Like the face he saw in the mirror in grade school. An East Indian face accept the cheekbones were higher.

The face he sometimes wished he could take off the Mask and be pale like his classmates who teased him.

No, Canada was not the country of his heritage. BUT <u>Canada is w*here his Birth took place*</u>, just like most of the rest of his classmates. He wanted to be accepted by everyone.

It was obvious this lad spent a lot of time in the sun, because he was even darker. Jack wondered "had the 3-hour journey out here given him too much time to reflect on past friendships? His need for family connection?"

It took him off guard at first. He swallowed the lump in his throat knowing the boy was waiting for his introduction.
Instead, Jack asked "What is your name son?"

The lad replied in a very official voice, much older than he looked:

**"Sir, I am Peetteri Pandora.
and remember Twin EEs; Twin TTs.
And within my name my father."**

He smiled gently, then placed his small hand sideways over the edge of his mouth as if to whisper a secret to Jack. Jack bent slightly down toward him – listening.

Quietly he whispered, "my mom says she named me after the Chickadee sound." And laughed like only uninhibited children can. "But I have no idea of the last part of the riddle."

With that, this little Peetteri 'Chickadee' had won Jack's admiration completely as he remembered his Butler duty.

"And what Sir, is yours?" The Official Voice again.
Jack took his card and handed it to Peetteri.

Peetteri red: "Jack Williams. Yes, of course, you have been expected."

Peetteri bowed his small body over his folded arm, and in the bow directed Jack to enter, the way an official Butler would. (barefoot and all) This amused Jack even more.

He wondered what the kid's mom must be like.

Or was it a Grandmother raising a grandchild?

No, the child said his mom named him.

He had no idea of how old the woman would be.

– that voice on the other end of the phone call.

Chapter 2

Dr. Henri Bokamosa & Dr. Marabella Karabo were Doctors on Vancouver Island, Canada. They loved their New Homeland with all the Beauty and Majesty an Island could offer.

They loved the Freedom of a Free Country. In South Africa, there was much unrest and resentment, that it was hard to study.

The Student Body had become very permissive.

– "take your *Pleasures* when you can, because who knows if it will be your last enjoyment." This became the Student Motto, whether a healthy one or not. Would they even be around to set up a practice in Medicine once they finished their long years of schooling and residency?

So many uncertainties!

When the opportunity came for a shift in continents, they jumped at the Unknown as being safer for their 2 small girls than the uncertainties of their known.

At least that is what they told each other was the reason.

Could they both be using this move as an escape from past secrets they held tight inside, even from the other? Perhaps the secrets kept them in top performance professionally. Deeply involved with their work, they had no time for much thought about what the purpose of life might be. Or even how they may have failed their own integrity. It was best that way. Who could question their dedication to their Patients!

They claimed their Profession as their Purpose as most humans do.

No, they had not neglected their children. As they began their Medical Careers, they shared a position at the hospital in Johannesburg so that one or the other was home with their small children.

Birthing 11 months apart, and in a young relationship, both Henri and Marabella agreed that two was enough with their exhausting careers. They had both hit 30 when Sara was born.

A couple of years later, they had bought a private practice and shared the responsibilities to accommodate growing girls and home. They were good parents according to their standards. Marabella, especially wanted a better home life for her children than she had herself. And that she thought "is yet another story."

They were upright Citizens, Church Goers. If someone had a medical need, they accommodated them whatever their skin. However, the unrest in their country undermined their confidence in working with everyone on an equal basis. So, of course the idea of living in a country where racial differences were accepted and accommodated was very appealing.

Though what country can rightly say that?

Freedom for their Girls – now 6 and 7.

Why not grasp opportunities as they presented. After all, this was almost too good to be True. Of course, the legalities take time, maybe years.

Chapter 3

Petra Karabo-Bokamosa, the oldest of two girls born in South Africa, emigrated to Canada when she was 8, almost 9 and grade 3.

Petra was told that even though she did not quite resemble parentage of Dutch descent in a strong way like Sara did, that she was a Love Child, conceived at Petra, Jordan. Therefore, her name. Petra was a place Henri and Marabella cherished. They loved the history and the architecture. And they seemed to love Petra, their eldest daughter, especially in early years.

EXCEPT for her Hair Out of Place!

Sometimes she questioned their love. I suppose as every child does, especially when they have workaholic parents and a 'spoiled' sibling. Often the love comes in monetary ways instead of listening ways. Or 'Be here NOW' ways.

Petra had a keen mind, a gentle child, perhaps a 'Crystal Child', sensitive to the moods and energy of people and all things around her. A Capricorn, always older than her years. She sensed the Essence of people's energy behind the *Tilted* Mask of perfection they tried to wear.

She loved the quiet of nature. She loved the sounds of the sea – the sounds you hear when you listen to a conch shell – when you put it up to your ear, and it is like you brought the ocean right on home with you. She loved the salty sea smell when they went to their cabin at the beach, which was seldom.

She had come to realize that the Seaside House was *'just a Status Symbol'* to her parents. They could say "yes, we have a home on the South Shores too". (actually, it was 'west coast' out of the way.) Petra wondered if 'the price was right' – something they could afford that claimed a 'Big Status Impression'.

Some years they did not go at all. They paid a contract person to check on the place and keep it fresh and safe. Her parents could hardly stand the gritty sand tracked in by their 'over-active' daughters let loose to nature. They preferred the Big Bus that most holidays were taken in. (and now Petra realized the motorhome was likely a Status thing as well). The Big Bus was too long to navigate the last 3 miles into the Property. If it could, chances are the Bus would be their accommodation out there instead of a cabin with few utilities.

Interesting how we see things differently when we are older and have experienced life. When we have removed some of the filters placed upon us by the *Status Quo, and the ADULTeration.*

We move beyond the ADULTeration of Social Expectations. We recognize the requirement of *Transparency.*

— "Trans Parent See."

Translated means: 'Beyond Adult See.'

No wonder she was "A Hair Out of Place" to her mother especially. Things were Black and White with mother. Even their house was decorated that way. Black, or maybe it was charcoal. No matter, lacking color and dulling of mind. Mother said it soothed her in the evening and quieted her nerves.

No wonder her father was always trying to *"Fix the Whole in HER Head"* from the other end. She simply did not fit their professional description. And then the fact that she looked very Asian Indian or even American Indian, did not settle well either.

Any mistake or misjudgement Petra made, she would hear the same thing: *"Come over here and let me fix that whole in your head"*. Whatever he meant; she did not understand. Well, he would Thump her head if not the other end.

Oh yes, she was a very obedient child, trying hard to keep peace. She did not like conflict of any kind. Mother and Father's constant debate irritated her. Of course, that was not the only sounds that irritated her. She was not like most teens either, who loved loud music and that chaotic beat. It all seemed to thump in her head and give her headaches.

'Rattle her brain' as she often expressed. She thought to herself 'And that is likely another Hair Out of Place to most people.'

Yes, Petra realized she was different. She was more Indian than the Dutch/British mix of her parents when she looked in the mirror. East or West she did not know exactly. Sara looked the part. *Petra did not.*

Reading, though she loved books, was a challenge. Yes, it did take a long time to read a page. By the time she was finished though, she understood it in more ways than most.

She read in pictures. Sometimes she wondered how many other people Read in Pictures.

And math? How could anyone figure it out the way this new school wanted students to figure it out was confusing and way beyond her. Adding, Subtracting, multiplication and even division were easy – she had the times tables memorized very well and especially the Trick of the 9s:

Simply make a list from 1-9; then start at the bottom and pretend you don't know 9x10, so you put a 0 after the 9=90. By the 8 place, 1=81; by the 7=72 and so on up the line. There you have the 9 times table. Easy!

Beyond Parent and school challenges, Her Heart Spoke. It even spoke about those challenges too. She listened carefully. This InnerNet Voice was a comforting friend when she had few other friends in a new land.

Yes, she realized now that she *'was a hair out of place and did not think like an intellectual Mind* in a very upstanding and professional environment.

Petra spent a lot of time trying to figure the other statement out: "Come over here and let me fix that whole in your head." It usually came in frustrated tones... She had no idea as to which way he thought that word was spelt Hole or Whole?

She giggled to herself 'and maybe he doesn't even know where the Whole might be'.

For herself, she had come up with the idea that The Whole was her own InnerNet. Maybe the Pineal Gland — the Antenna to the Wisdom beyond ourselves.

Things in growing up seemed dark enough. She needed COLOR and lots of it. Gardens and Parks provided the color her home did not. Fortunately, there were a lot of parks and the long season provided a lot of Blooms.

Libraries and Book Stores supplied the food Imagination Feasts upon. Petra educated herself as to Quantum Physics, even before it was known as that. Through Books and her own InnerNet, she simply understood that Everything was Energy in Motion. Everything vibrated. Just hold a stone or two of different colors and you can feel the vibration difference.

She KNEW!

Another thing Petra knew that many others did not, was the value of LOVE (Capital LOVE). The kind that 'GOD IS LOVE' means. She preferred 'Creator is LOVE' as she did not hear anyone bad mouthing Creator. She sure did *God,* and it made her sad.

One day at the Public Library, a book literally fell off the shelf and into her lap. It was a big book. Petra took note because Books do not just fall into your lap. After renewing her borrow time, a couple of times, she knew this Book was as important to her as her Bible in which she hid the photo of 'the man with long braids'.

She noted the price of the Book. Went to her Allowance Bank, and off to The Book Store she went. Petra was fourteen at the time.

One day she would study something in the Bible. The next she would study something in 'A Course in Miracles'. **ACIM** helped her bring more LOVE into what she read in the Bible. ACIM helped her see her responsibility for her own actions and life.

Yes, things happen outside of our control, but she learned:

"We always have the control over our own ATTITUDE. The way we think about the situation."

But we may not think we have control of our attitude because it is a Learned Control.

Yes, she was 'a hair out of place' as a teen. And so, she might be considered an Introvert; even though a good conversation from the heart was something she craved. Most people were shallow and wore masks of what they thought they should be, instead of BEING WHO THEY WERE CREATED TO BE.

She could not even have a visit about the deep things of heart with her parents. They were too deep for their indoctrination with money, pharmaceuticals, and being successful. Man-made stuff and man-made chemical solutions she saw as being no solution at all as she grew older. Maybe she saw it that way, because she was 'old for her grade' after moving to Canada.

Her Parent's definition of success was Money, Possessions equal Status. Whereas she saw it like Thoreau saw it:

'Wealth is the ability to fully experience Life.'

Her depth of conversation was deep beyond the shallows most people wanted to go. *"How's the weather"* did not cut it for her. Most seemed fearful of speaking from the heart. They seemed to fear what might come out if they allowed themselves to get quiet and express their true feelings.

By the time she was fifteen, she understood the Statistics that over 90% of our uncontrolled thoughts are negative and maybe not even our own. (whose voice does it sound like?) About that time, before the Utah Olympics, a survey claimed that 83% of people hated winners. 17% liked winners.
In studying the work of Dr. David Hawkins and 'The Levels of Consciousness' she understood that 78% of the population dwells in a negative energy and likes to have it that way. As if they are the Victim instead of understanding they are the creator of their own creation or more commonly know as our circumstances and situation.

These people can not stand SILENCE. Petra loved silence. Just think all they are missing. In the SILENCE is where she learned so much that mattered in living.

In her head, she wondered what a World that turned the 80/20 Rule on its head would be like? To think in a way that only 20% of thoughts went negative and 80% were positive. She would be her own Experiment! She would listen more carefully to how she was talking to herself.

Books rather than TV, Movies or teen music were her style. A Book, you could carry off to a quiet space and become whatever your imagination saw the words to be, the sounds, the smell – all the senses could be involved and choose what they would.

The other stuff dictated what it was that you were to be seeing. The background noise in a movie often dictated something the action in the movie did not.

They confused and confounded her own InnerNet. Her Creative Imagination wanted to do the imaging for herself. She could keep it cool and non-violent. She could keep a quietness her own InnerNet could hear and appreciate every descriptive word.

Oh, *maybe it was the yelling in the streets, the shots and the rape that caused her to choose this quietness instead?*

Now that might be something to explore too! Sometime. Maybe she had secrets no one should know just like her parents did. Someday when she was older, maybe an adult, she would understand that '*deep guilt and fear*' she felt, that depressed her, and yet she could not understand why.

Her life was good.

Before they moved to Canada, and her parents left their study books in South Africa, she would sneak off to the attic and rummage through those books and the old photos from their college days. They were actual photos and not on someone's digital device. It must have been the last year before they left, that a photo fell out of a Biology Text – well, more than 1 did. Petra recognized her mother, but not the man in the photo with her that had long black braids.

On the back, it said "Love You Always, Ben Parker". There was a resemblance to herself – especially the higher cheekbones. She liked the Braids too. Must be a symbolic style because boys with long hair at that time did not keep it that tidy. (From this photo, she considered herself west Indian as it was American Indians that history had pictures of with braided hair.)

Probably against the RULES, but Petra tucked that photo in her little Bible. No one would suspect where it had gone, and chances are it would never be missed. There was also a photo of her mom on the beach with this man; but she dares not steal more than one, and besides, if Daddy found it in her Bible, or if it fell out, Mommy might have to explain. That could make for another argument.

Petra enjoyed a good conversation about the different philosophies of life. Her parents told her to be careful of what she was studying, when they knew she had bought her own copy of the Complete Book 'A Course in Miracles', because it might not line up with *what we are supposed to believe from the Bible Christian life.*

Humm! She did not see them living what they read to their daughters in the Bible when they were small children. She did not see the Higher thought patterns the Book was teaching her in their living of it. So, what were they afraid of?

Yes, as a family they had watched "The Secret Documentary" together. Her parents thought it would help them be better people and get what they wanted of man-made things and wealth. To Petra it appeared to be more about Getting Stuff and begging God for Idols instead of BEING the kind of person that automatically has the Virtues to wisely use the stuff when it comes to us. But then she was probably about 8 when they watched it. It was before they left Africa. Yes, her parents were not prejudice and they would describe themselves as Church goers.

Everything changed when they came to Canada when they moved away from Daddy's Bokamosa family. Other than going to Church on Sunday, Bible interaction never happened at home. BUT Petra wondered, *'was Church just a way of showing your Patients that you had right principles too?* She saw their Church experience as accommodating their clients – keeping everybody happy.

– *"My Doctor goes to the same Church I do."*

Anyway, as she grew older, none of that mattered. **She was traveling a different path to most who closed their minds to their own potential.**

Her Connection to a Creator of LOVE was in the Wilds – out beyond the sounds of the city and the booming music some neighbours seemed to like sharing. Petra preferred **the quiet where she could HEAR her own quiet InnerNet as she liked to call it.**

The Big Book ACIM & the Holy Bible were her friends. They spoke of what she felt in her heart. Church sermons often did not. And she did not often see the adults living what was preached – *in word only.*

She did not need Dr. Google, or even Dr. Bokamosa and Dr. Karabo. She was quite content learning from nature and books that inspired her to LOVE more; to live in Gratitude. Something she saw truly little of at home.

Now do not get me wrong, people love in a capacity, at least, according to their own interpretation and *challenged ability to love.*

Like a wise *aunty* at church, that had become her friend, once told her as she complained about her parents' constant debate over patient care, money matters, childcare and a host of other conflicting opinions – this

'Aunty' said: **"Petra, some people love deeply with their hands around each other's throat."**

Now that was a different perspective for her keen eyes and ears. Physically, she realized her eyes and ears were sharper than most, therefore, more sensitive.

She decided to allow her parents their differences, and live her own integrity, which seemed vastly different than hers.
And maybe that is "A hair out of place" and "A whole in her head" to them too. Maybe that is why Daddy's strong Dutch heritage is always trying to force his dominant thinking on her.

He is a well-trained professional. Petra saw that the Pharma-Feudalism had him as a Peasant even though he did not see it for himself. He did not know it, but she stopped taking his prescriptions long ago. They only dulled her creative mind and gave her a lot of unwanted thoughts she had to sort through.

Mother was not quite that enslaved to pharmaceuticals. Maybe that is why they argue so much over patient care. One prescribes, the other looks for alternatives within the system.

Appearance was more important to Mother. You would wonder at it being so, when you go through photo albums and boxes and see the rebellion she had – something like Sister Sara for sure.

Mother found it more important that her girls look perfect. And since she always claimed Petra had unruly hair, Petra's hair was kept noticeably short. Sometimes Petra wondered if she looked more like a boy than a girl.

If she could do it herself, she would have a long braid down the back of her head.

But then maybe she had fallen in Love with mother's old boy friend. She searched every detail in the photo often enough. Then again, maybe that would remind mother of her past and there would be more friction between herself and her mother.

As mother said
– **"leave dead lions buried".**

Chapter 4

Sara Mayana Bokamosa was born when Petra was 11 months old. Sara was a beautiful curly haired blonde child. Her hair was not as curly as her father's, but none the less the long blonde curls were very appealing. Daddy once explained Sara's beauty as 'rare' – Not many Blonde people had Brown Eyes.

Soon she became known as the 'Wild Child'. She had a mind of her own, determined to live from her own EGO. Part of it maybe the strong attachment both parents had toward her. Sara soon learned that she had her parents wrapped around her little finger so to speak and could get whatever she wished.

She often blamed Petra for the scratches and accidents around the house. Every ones everything seemed to belong to her. Even when they went visiting, she would bring home whatever she liked. When it was reported missing, or found at home, she would pass it off as if it were Petra that brought it home. Sara seemed to delight in Daddy "Fixing the Whole in Petra's Head."

Whereas Petra saw things that needed to be done and did them to relieve her parents of some things she could do; Sara ignored them.

It was like she was 'Princess and you best serve me'.

She was very much a 'Get Me' child. And since most of the Doctors' Love came through stuff, Sara was good at getting stuff even though it did not make or keep her happy for long.

She was an early riser. She had energy that kept everyone on their toes to keep up. However, when she began pre-school, she had a problem fitting in and doing what the teachers told the class to do.

Having Doctor parents, it was not long before she began to have her morning *'cocktail'* to keep her calm at school. Yes, there was a noticeable difference.

And 'here Sara is your yummy before bed'.

Now the problem was waking her up and getting her off to school on time. But the one thing parents agreed upon was that they could keep track of her much better when she was medicated. She was not so exhausting for them. But she was then a grumpy child.

Maybe she just needed 'Happy Pills added!'

Chapter 5

Henri & Marabella met on a University arranged Tour of the Holy Land a week after finishing Medical School and a month before their jobs at the Hospital in Johannesburg started. It was an opportunity for students to take added credits.

The Topic "The Modern Science behind Ancient Medicines".
Their lives had not crossed until this Journey. They had gone to different Medical Schools and grown up as far as east is from west in South Africa. On the flight from Johannesburg to Petra, Jordan, fate placed them as seat mates.

As they compared notes, and histories, they began to become very attracted to each other. Marabella, being a bit of what was called 'a hippy' the child of that generation, was perhaps a bit like her second daughter later was.

Henri was fascinated by Marabella's Free Spirit.

He felt a little trapped in the strong religious background he grew up in. And maybe the freedom of Marabella, gave him freedom as well. Not only were they seat mates on the plane, but they also found they would be working in the same department at the same Hospital when they got back to Johannesburg. How cool was that!

Henri's studies took him into Gynecology. Marabella's studies took her into Delivery and preemie care. What a Combo they thought. AND future planning, they decided that their training would work well together should they decide to have their own Practice.

Their Class days were short at Petra. Assignments required exploration and research at the library archives as well as hikes around the area – a study of the Frankincense Trail etc. There was little reason for them to be apart.

Their hikes and exploration soon became that of each other as well. It was not hard to collapse into either her Dorm Room or his when others were out and about. However, their first experience came way to soon and unexpected. The second day they were in Jordan. They were taken by Bus to the Dead Sea for a mineral bath.

The choice was also given, if you wished to stay longer, and could afford it, you could stay 2 extra nights enjoying the minerals with an assignment to take note of the effects on the anatomy and mind. There was a Bedouin Camp of Tent accommodations for the price. The tour bus would be back on the third day to transport back to Petra.

There were shelters as change rooms. For some reason they found themselves changing together. Sex was not an unfamiliar territory for either of them. And there it was right before them for the indulgence thereof. Delicious it was before wondering out into the Saltiest Water they had ever experienced. They decided to split the cost and stay the extra days. This was way too good an opportunity to study the Dead Sea and the effects it could have on their body, mind, and future.

Three weeks fly by very quickly when you are having fun!
By the time they boarded the plane back to Johannesburg, Marabella was quite sure she was pregnant. Her regular monthly did not show up. She had an almost constant nausea ever since the day at the Dead Sea. Henri was aware of her discomfort. How could he not be when they

spent so much time together. Yet it was not a morning thing or even vomit – it simply was.

Would this be the end of their Budding Relationship? That was the question Marabella would ask herself when she was alone in the Girl's Dorm. She wondered if Henri was thinking the same. From his studies, did he recognize the symptoms? Or would he be condemning her for letting it happen? She remembered the woman that was caught in adultery and brought to Jesus. The man was no where in sight. It was all about *the 'woman's sin'*. In her changing hormonal state, the tears would come, and she would berate herself for being so dumb. But how could it happen? Had she forgotten to take The Pill? When did she miss taking it? Did the Dead Sea water counteract the Pill's effect? Do most women get morning sickness this fast? Or maybe they had it so often the last week that her hormones were not keeping up?

No, it could not be morning sickness. The queasy tummy was with her all day. Maybe it was just the excitement and different foods than she was used to. Whatever, she had found in Henri, he was what she referred to as a 'Keeper'.

She did not want to think of the Prof anymore. Obviously, he was a passing experience – one that causes a person to look even deeper into themselves and recognize what it is you genuinely want? He was a deep thinker she could not always understand. He made things possible for her in University she could not on her own. He got her into classes and electives she had no right to be in.

Sad but too much 'class and country difference'. Too much age difference – like 12 years is a Big Deal when you are in your 20s and he in his 30s almost 40! Yes, they had said their forever 'Goodbye' the night before she flew to Johannesburg and this amazing next chapter in the journey with Henri.

Marabella practiced – I will inform Henri in the morning that he will be a wonderful father to a Petra Child – the Blessing of our union forever. Life is good! And she fell asleep.

Henri had asked for seating together on the flight back to what would be their home in Johannesburg. He would have the privilege of introducing his Beloved to his home city and to the hospital of his Residency. It would all be new territory for Marabella. Through the internet, Marabella had found a nice inexpensive suite close to the hospital. Henri would return to his family's home – where he had never left for long. At least they would be close to each other and working together.

Once the flight was in the air, and leveled out, along with Marabella's tummy; she decided it was time to break the news to Henri. She took a very deep breath, and began "Henri, I trust you will be excited to know we will be Parents? Soon it will expose itself."

Henri was silent for nearly half an hour. Marabella wondered if she had blown them apart. And then she corrected herself – had The News, the being Honest blown him away?

Finally, Henri reached over and took Marabella's hands in his. He was sideways in his seat. She had the window seat for which she was glad. Whatever was about to come out of Henri would be relatively private.

Henri said "Marabella, my love, will you marry me?" Marabella's parents were never married. But then again, it had not lasted forever like Henri's parent's union did.

Slowly, Marabella said "do we need to go that far? You could just come and live in the Apartment with me. It is close to the hospital?"

"No" Henri said. "That will not work in my family. A Christian man takes responsibility for his doings and looks after his family in a respectable way." He could see that Marabella was a little uncomfortable with this statement. She was a Free thinker and saw Church as restrictive. He gave her space for thinking it through.

Finally, he broke the silence between them. "Marabella, we are consenting adults. We are free to make choices, not only for ourselves, but for what is best for <u>our baby</u>."

He was not blaming her for somehow missing her Pill or trusting the Pill when it is only 97% accurate. She caught the softness in which he said, "our baby". He was taking responsibility for this Embryo as well as she.

(Neither one of them had the slightest thought of aborting. With his practice, he had every right and every technique to eliminate this inconvenience for them. They both knew because it was in their training manual that abortion is not the answer. It is a sure ride into depression, sometimes incurable.)

The nervous system remembers and presents feelings of guilt.

It is true that his beliefs about life were different than hers. But he did have a point in "the baby being ours" and "doing what is right for "our baby". He was not classifying her as a '*sinner woman*' though his family may. She had no idea about them. They probably did not have any secrets to hide. She was very new to his culture.

"If I say Yes, how soon will it be?"

"But what if we don't match up once we have children? What if our hospital shifts never allow us to be together? Henri, I have so many 'what ifs."

Henri simply said "My Marabella, we will work through the hard stuff. God, fate, karma, whatever you want to call it, brought us together in very unexpected ways and circumstances. We both know that we went into our relationship with less than pure credentials. We both know that we believe in having been created Equal – Male and Female created He them. We are both Doctors of equal standing. We can, with the help of Heaven, work through the hard stuff."

"Yes, we do have student debt to pay off. Yes, we do have a Family in the Incubator (as he gently placed his hand on her still flat belly). And Yes, there are a lot of details to sort out. But I, Henri Bokamosa, am committed to our future as a family." He chuckled – 'my last name means 'future'. No point in delaying it."

"You are right Dr. Henri 'Future'."

"I, Dr. Marabella Karabo (and mine means 'by accident') do accept your offer of a 'Happily Ever after' whatever shape that takes." With that, he leaned even farther forward and placed a gentle kiss on her temple, as he whispered in her ear "I love you Marabella Karabo-Bokamosa."

"I love you tiny Petra Karabo-Bokamosa, whoever you BE." As he patted her tummy. Henri took her right hand in his left and leaned back on his own seat with a long deep breath. You asked earlier "How long?"

"My reply to that is immediately. No, it will not be a fancy wedding as such. Probably that is not in our budget anyway." He chuckled and she liked the sound of his chuckles.

"You might say we are returned from the Honeymoon – yah!"
"We can throw the party for our first Anniversary or something like that."

"My suggestion, and hopefully you agree, is that we stop by the Legal Office on our way home after we land. The paperwork is the important part – the legalities you know."

"My brother is dropping a car off at the airport this morning on his way to work. We can load into it and take stuff to your apartment. Then we can take our passports, birth certificates etc. to the Law Office that my

Buddy Thato owns. He will do the documents up quickly for us from texted information I will send before us."

"Going to my folks house Married is the best reception for you. They trust my better judgement." And so that is how it went on their return to Johannesburg, South Africa as A Husband & Wife Team – a vow of equality.

Chapter 6

At 29, I, Jamie Gillette Parker am sitting on the deck overlooking the cove, reminiscent of my life –

Like a Diamond in The Master's hand, each facet different and yet alike, each reflecting the brilliance of the Sun in iridescent flame.

I am moved to admire the Bokamosa Diamond Ring on my finger – the 3 small Diamonds flashing their Light. I shall never forget that day that Peter Bokamosa Sr. took Peter Jr. and I to the Mine. Probably the last day before his office was moved home. But that is for another chapter. This is meditation time.

I love this quiet time of the morning when all there is, *is the Creator and I to converse*. This time is like a Flow of Gratitude I offer to my Creator that flows back to me, as if my praise for being Created was well accepted and Creation thanks me for thanking its Energy, for Living its LOVE Essence from within to without.

A Beautiful Song that continues through out a long Eternity – a Song that always was and always will be. In Christ, (Creator's LOVE exemplified) I have become 'the LOVE I am looking for'.

No, it was not always so.

It was not always this way with me. So much turmoil and confusion of events and adult influences – adults stuck in their own Emotional Prisons, unwilling to become transparent and vulnerable. To me, Transparent and Vulnerable are Essential to Emotional Harmony from within to without.

I am quite alright being alone with my son; and he with me, though I suspect a man's influence is a positive thing on his. Fortunate for him that the Big Building Project developed.

Fortunate for me that Jack, the Architect has taken him under his wing, and allowed him to participate in the project. He is learning a lot of 'Hands On' stuff I have no idea of how to teach.

But still, it would be nice to share so much Beauty in life with someone to communicate it to in a Human Body; like I mean a Male that loves the things I love. An equal partnership with all of Creation – someone who does not kick the dog or the cat and can Ho'oponopono people rather than share their critical analysis about political people and anyone else.

I am so grateful that I learned this valuable Hawaiian technique. I wonder how many times it saved me from being a *complete basket case*.

Yes, I have received a Fortune unexpected. I do not want to make the mistake of taking someone's 'love per say' that is just here for an easy ride and the money like Mara's gardener. And maybe even Mara herself.

I am Abundant in all my living even when it comes to relationships. I am sensitive to my InnerNet. So, I shall TRUST I will make wise decisions when it comes to relationships of HEART too.

We have had a few fellows around over the past 2 years. I do like to notice each one and observe to see if they match my Inner Criteria. Yes, I agree that I am choosey. <u>It is required.</u>

We have the rest of our lives on the table. I plan to live LOVE fully, from a Heaven here on Earth concept. Why wait for something beyond death when we can start our enjoyment of it here and now? Back to the "At ONE ment", The Atonement of Eden's first Garden.

Yes, current events are sometimes crazy; but I do not require indulgence in fake news. Thankfully! I have this Beautiful Space I call home now. And within this Beautiful Space, a place called Heart with a strong InnerNet Connection, from which to choose attitudes that align with Heaven.

Yes, of course I have Willow Wisdom, who has taught me so much; but it would be nice to have a special man who completes the procreative loop. Should we wish to have another child, my time is slowing down. But then, I am only as old as my parents when they had me and then my sister.

My son's grandparents were probably even older when they had his father. (Fortunately, Naomi taught me that I could choose the 'Story' I wished to talk about Peter (Peetteri) Benjamin Parker's conception.) And so, I did. Yes, I combined my recollections of Petri and Peter jr.

Life is a matter of perceptions, after all.

Would I ever find that Special Somebody who would BE the Diamond around my finger? The wonders of Peter and Petri's gentle LOVE; and maybe Grandad's gentleness and generosity as well, all wrapped up in ONE amazing Romantic.

Maybe not. I am a Mother with child. Men want a woman, but not necessary her family and baggage. I knew it would have to be someone who loved my son as much as he loves me.

Someone who would forget that Peter was not their flesh and blood. AND with this relatively secluded Lifestyle, who could I meet? Unless of course he is one of the Authors who chooses this Reclusive Place to write a Book. Or someone who rents the facility for their own Frolic Retreat. At least we would have some areas of mind and heart in harmony.

The past 2 years have been busy ones. Yes, I have lots of male contact right now, with all the Tradesmen doing all that this Jack fellow is ordering up. Jack is kind of sweet. I also know this is 'business' I will not let my heart-mind get into this. Not yet at least. But I cannot help but notice similarities to someone special from the past.

Yes, and this Jack fellow seems to have a real interest in my son. I must admit, they do look a lot alike – one in a full-grown body. The other in a steadily growing body.

The first time Jack was out, after the business was settled; he said he had a half hour to spare, so he grabbed a soccer ball out of the back of his RAV and down to the beach Jack and my boy went. I really did enjoy the sight.

Peter must get kind of bored living with a Mom and no Dad to tussle with. I still wonder if Jack has a small family or not? I think he must, to know how to tussle with Peter. He also includes Peter in every stage of the construction here. He knows Peter is home schooled. What an excellent 'work experience' for my son!

Every time Jack rolls out the Blueprints, he gets Peter to join him and explains what is going to be done next. And yes, Peetteri now has his own Hard Hat and leather tool belt, which he wears every day. Jack's gift to Peetteri for his sixth Birthday. Another Thankful that I could not have imagined on my own.

Jamie might be a boyish name, but I am not a rough and tumble. Tomboy of sort, but not boy ruff.

I giggle every time I say Peetteri, which is often. What ever inspired me to place 'Twin EEs, Twin TTs? My immaturity and my love of nature I suppose. Maybe Willow's native influence at the time of his birth as well. But I was wise enough to place it as a Second name – Peter Peetteri Benjamin Parker. I notice that Jack calls him Peter now. Maybe I should too, now that he is becoming a little man.

Chickadee was the 1st Bird that spoke to me when I awakened that first morning 'Alone! Without family! Yet 'with Child.'

Let us clarify that. I heard Willow Wisdom, a mid aged native lady in the kitchen. A woman I had never met before. And yet a LOVE Sent Comforter when I arrived in the wee hours of mid-night after an exceptionally long flight.

(The Uber Driver had told me it was arranged for Willow, the woman whose Autistic son kept the cabin in good order, would be waiting to care for me. But all of that is for a future chapter. A chapter that Peter Sr. saw no value in keeping; **and changed the plan against my parents wishes.**)

That Peetteri sound like the Chickadees I love makes me happy. They often call 'Peetteri! Peetteri! Peetteri!' especially before a storm. I love that sound, a little haunting in its resonance. It cheers me in our woodland home with few human voices to mar the resonance. And I remember:

All of Nature is a Symphony of Praise if we listen.

I am all Country Girl! And really, does it matter that someone should cherish me 'happily ever after'? I am so connected to My Integrity InnerNet, what more could I require? I am confident that the All-Seeing, Eternal LOVE Source created:

From LOVE,

In LOVE,

To be LOVED

To BE LOVE

To be LOVEABLE and

To be LOVE-ABLE.

If we are not the LOVE we are looking for, no one else's love will satisfy us.

"When this Man comes my way,

<u>he had better be his own Best Friend First</u>".

Chapter 7

Jack Williams has become a name to take notice of on Vancouver Island. An Architect that stands behind his word.

Jack drove his Cherry Red, RAV4 Sport out of town to the west side of the island, to a coastal property on the Pacific Shore. He was looking forward to some 'Think Time'. It was at least a 3-hour trip. He had brought his backpack just in case he saw a place he wished to hike on the way back. His tent was always in the back. On a Holiday Island, you never know when you will find a spot that 'claims you for 24-hours.'

He reflected on how good life had turned his way in 5 short years of **'Jack Williams Architect Inc.**

His mother had died the third year of University. She was 72. Same age as his father had been when he passed just before Jack left grade school for Junior high. He had never thought about how old his parents were when he was born. They had come to Canada shortly after his brother was born. They were Research Professors studying Marine Biology.

Jack was born a year and 9 months after his brother's high school graduation. Now he thought - *'that must have been a Huge Surprise!'*

Now that his education was behind him. Now that his financial future was in place and doing well, he wondered if it might be time for a Long-Term relationship followed by Family? After all life was passing him very quickly. A lot of folks already have their family growing at 32. He did not want to be 'Old Parents' for young children. He had done a lot on his own. His father passing when he was twelve. That left his mother, in her mid fifties a single parent. Always tired!

Jack was on his own a lot as a child. His brother had gone to Georgia for University before he was born. (Actually, he did not even know if his brother was alive. Eight years ago, they failed to locate him when his mother died.)

With both his parents being gone, he decided there was no reason why he could not change his name to something more Acceptable than a 'petri dish' as an Architect. Petri might be a good Biologist name, but Architect? That was the beginning of Jack Williams. Officially all documentation bore that name.

Jack began to reminisce about the few relationships with a woman he had allowed himself to have. He decided to start with his school years. He remembered Grade 3 when Rosy and he hid under the bleachers and experienced their 'first kiss'. He had to chuckle to himself as he thought of their innocence and the taste of her lips. He remembered she tasted a lot like Spearmint – he wondered if she was chewing Wrigley's?

Junior High brought all the hormones to the surface. How embarrassing it was when a guy really had to work at controlling the bump in his pants when he talked to a girl. Girl's bumps could grow and be up front. They even made clothing to accent their bumps. But then again, their bumps did not rise and shrink like his. His had a life of its own that he really did not understand back then especially at the sight of those female bumps, and of course it was not something parents told you much about, especially an old mother.

He knew Jenny liked him a lot. She was a good dancer. They matched steps pretty much right on. But he thought she liked him too much to be a girl friend. Afterall, how could a guy control his urges with someone who wanted to take you to bed.

<u>He had principle.</u>

He wanted a Sacred Friend – one that he could visit with and talk about all kinds of things without all the hormonal play. Afterall, he knew from what his older parents were that hormones only last so long.

He wondered where these girls had moved to. How their lives panned out? Were they happy in what they had chosen?

Ya gotta have a girl who knows how to communicate from the heart, with a BIG HEART! Sex wears out like the pair of shorts that holds it in does.

His Girl would have to be HIS.

Jack grew noticeably quiet in his thoughts. A tear rolled down his cheek. He tried to hold back, *"big boys don't cry"* how often had he heard that growing up?

For goodness sake! What is the matter? What does it matter that a man cry?

Are emotions supposed to be imprisoned to explode in other ways? Why are women allowed to talk about emotions when men are supposed to talk about sports? He could care less about competitive sports. He often heard the office girls conversing about their feelings. Even embracing and sharing tears at times when it was necessary.

Jack pulled off at the next pull-out. Somehow, he needed to get himself together before he made this house call. Why was he so emotional anyway? He got out and stretched by the side of the highway.

And then he realized his deepest attachment to any Girl was Petra. Even her name matched his own before he thought an Architect should have a more British name; especially if it was going to be a Business name. Petri Raju just did not make the cut.

But here Jack Williams stood on the side of the road as vehicles passed by. Here he was back in the Petri Raju body with the Beautiful Petra Karabo-Bokamosa! She resembled his nationality in a lot of ways, but her high cheek bones expressed more of an American Aboriginal – he had even taken it upon himself to investigate the different tribes and study the photos and paintings to see if he could identify her nationality.

He wondered if she had been adopted because she was not the Dutch of her parents or sister in look. He had to admit though that some families have a 'flashback' to a nationality some were in history. Petra looked very much like the Sioux of the Midwest, lower central Canada, and the Dakotas. Maybe a Lakota.

He could still smell the scent of cedar in her hair. How he had come to LOVE that Girl in a Capital way. How he wished that whatever his name was now, he could somehow contact her and see if she were attached or still a possibility – HIS GIRL!

The Library of the high school was there general meeting station when they were not in classes. **But where oh where was she now?**

The Monday after her graduation, she flew back to South Africa for University. He flew out an hour later in the opposite direction for his third year of University in England. Her parents wanted her to be *a Well-Trained Doctor* to take over their practice. She was such a kind and gentle person; he was sure she would be a good one; though he doubted she could ever cut into anyone or even give injections she was so gentle.

They had so many visits and talked about so many topics in that year before he left for University. They even studied some of the same books – 'A Course in Miracles' was a common topic.

In fact, it was that coincidentally that got their Attention – both sat down at the same table with the same book. It was a book to study, much like the Bible, but from a Quantum Field approach. It made a lot of sense to them both.

So, they decided to study a lesson a day. Of course, they never got through them all because the year was too short. Jack wondered if she still had the book and studied it. He knew she liked it so much she had bought her own copy. And likewise, he had his own too.

When he was home for holidays, he always looked her up, and they would talk about his studies, what university life was like, what life really meant, what they really wanted from life. The Important things that you find few people willing to become Transparent about.

By the time of her graduation, he understood well, that she was between a rock and a hard spot. She knew she did not want to be a doctor, with all the long hours her parents had. And all the deceptions and prescriptions. She genuinely wanted to develop her artistic skills – she was Very Good!

He had a painting she did just for him. It was an early painting, as she gave it to him for his graduation – a gift to remember her by when their ways no longer criss-crossed.

It was a stretched canvas within a wooden hoop – like a Dream Catcher that could catch the light from every direction. Both sides were painted. The first side was of a Brave and a Beautiful Maiden. Almost as if it were a 'self portrait' of the two of them.

Above and Behind them was 'the Great Spirit' over shadowing. Below them was a Cougar with watchful eyes – The Protector.

36

The Brave and Maid are facing each other with hands turned up, hers upon his, as if waiting for them to be filled from above. They are elbows bent apart. He a Feather Headdress, and she has a large and a small feather along with a Wild Rose to the side of her long hair. (Petra's hair was always extremely short, but he could imagine her with long hair like the painting.)

Turn the painting over, and the couple stand close together with a papoose in their arms. They are both looking upon the little one with great admiration.

The Great Spirit is still above and behind them and the cougar just under the papoose. If you raise the painting to the light, both sides are faintly visible. The Spirit and the Cougar match perfectly. The Papoose Couple fit nicely between the Couple on the other side, like their arms support the Papoose as well.

The painting was easily packed with him in a nice flat box. It hangs in front of his bedroom window now to catch the light. Of course, she also wove sparkly beads to catch the light, and feathers hang from the bottom. He thought of all the hours of work and LOVE she put into that Work of Art. **Just for HIM!**

And then sadly he gifted her a break in his own Integrity – never mind her Integrity. He had two years of university behind him. She had asked him to be her Escort for Grad. He missed nearly a week of classes to be there for her. He was not a bit sorry about it either. Perhaps he had negligently left her with a broken heart. He made no further contact.

However, there was a twinge of regret that sometimes haunted him. He was so busy with studies and life, why did he not think about getting her address or even email so they could keep a connection. Why did he take it for granted that she would always be there when he came back to the Island, waiting to pick up where they left off?

Her Graduation was several years past now. Even though she was 'Of Age' to choose, she was sent back to Johannesburg her father's city for university. And highly likely she was still over there. Maybe even happily married. She was an excellent specimen in so many ways.

THE GUY IS LUCKY! LUCKY! LUCKY!

How was he to know?

And "Sadly I missed the catch of a lifetime" he thought.

Since he moved back and started his business, he noticed that her parents Practice had been sold. He noticed that someone else lived in their house. It was not that he did not try to find her again. But it seemed to lack the opportunity to meet any of her family and ask about her. He had heard that her sister Sara had died very suddenly not long after Petra's grad. Little else did he know. With that, he sighed deeply and decided he had best put things aside and get on with the work he had set out to do.

Right now, he decided it was not something he wanted to look at. It might be too deep. "This is a Workday and must be done." With that he got back into the RAV and turned on the signal light to pull back into the traffic along the mountain road. He still had an hour to drive. He decided to stop the thinking and simply take in the awesome scenery.

And so, that was the beginning of Jack Williams.

Chapter 8

Jamie - In this morning's meditation I recognize Confidence and Humility walk hand in hand.

Confidence is something I recognize that I do not have on my own. Instead, I am Amazed at the Magic of Humility the Integrity InnerNet brings to rejoice in.

I am not the Painter of the Picture.

I am not the Writer of the Book.

I am not the Presenter of the Frolic.

I am not the Lifestyle Coach encouraging LOVE.

Yes, I am constantly Amazed at what is Presented, whether in Painting, in the Book, or in the Coaching Session. I learn things I did not know I knew in each session. My Client's issues bring out something from the InnerNet that often resonates with something within me. And I thank them for their Confidence in my InnerNet Connection. If Dr David Hawkins is correct, few people indulge in the Quiet that opens the InnerNet to us.

I am simply Downloading the Magic that comes in living a LOVE Life from within to without. I could not tell you why I said what I did in the book, or even why/how the characters live in the Book. I could not replicate a painting, or even teach you the techniques used in the painting. ***They JUST ARE!***

The Quiet Mind creates Availability in us to allow the InnerNet to reveal the Magic. The same can be said of you, Dear Reader when you become a Friend - Owning Integrity Quiet InnerNet. The connection subscription is FREE!

It is said that over 90% of our uncontrolled thoughts are negative. A survey before the Utah Olympics stated that 83% of people surveyed did not like winners. No wonder we all have little confidence. No wonder the World is more in a state of vengeance than LOVE.

By getting to know our InnerNet we can frolic in changing the state of our thoughts, thinking, and become more in Tune to have 90% of our thinking <u>positive and LOVE</u> oriented.

When Willow and I have our own 3 Day Frolic, or at someone else's, and we do the 'Behind Your Back Process'; there are always at least 2 'Confident' on the card that hangs on my back.

Oh! Apologies: I thought everyone knew this Process. Well since you do not dear Reader, everyone gets a large Index Card on a string that goes around the neck and hangs at the back. Everyone has a marker and prints the first word that comes to mind about the person on the card on their back. It is a Confidence Builder.

Often the Tribe has known each other for less than 2 or 3 days. A remarkably interesting Process that never fails to encourage me, whether I am the Presenter or Attending another Presenter's Classes.

If self-confidence matches the Humility Confidence that comes from our own InnerNet, it is often misunderstood at first, until the relationship grows to see that 'this person's Confidence is coming from The Deep.

However, there is a self-confidence that is anything but humble but rather conceited. "I am a Self Made." The I DID IT myself personality.

The Narcistic personality. All people we want to Run Away From. Their Mask is scary.

Sadly, sometimes the Confidence that comes from True Humility is thought of as the above.

Owning Integrity and living LOVE soon dispels that assumption. The Mask is not there. There is nothing they can pull off or peek under.

The Truth of our InnerNet is ALL THERE IS.

We as Humans sometimes see <u>humiliation</u> as being the thing that brings a humble spirit.

I see humiliation as being the very thing that brings rebellion or depression. (Willow and I have had a good conversation about this. She sees it this way too.) It has happened a lot with our Clients. We see it as they relate their story to us.

"If you are telling me I can't do/say that; that is exactly what I am going to do." OR "I can't please them no matter how I try. Nothing I say is right." Paralyzed into a silent depression, and then the humiliator wonders WHY?

Humiliation does nothing but reveal a hidden hurt in the humiliator.

A LOVE response can gently reveal or uncover the humiliator - bully's underlying issue and encourage them to get rid of what is bothering them from within their own Being. Can polish the Connection to the InnerNet for them.

This is True Humility. This is True Confidence that comes from a strong connection to the InnerNet.

The only Truth is Eternal LOVE. Being Confident in Eternal LOVE brings Confidence that shines Humility.

Chapter 9

'City was not her map.
Social Quo was not her style.
Look what it did for her Parents.
Look what it did for her sister.
All were gone now.
She was alone with a small son.'

Jamie recognized she was again receiving The Story – 'You've Got a Hair Out of Place' and must get back to the computer.

Willow Wisdom, the Medicine Woman down the lane from her had become her 'Chosen Family'. It was Willow who was at the Cabin with a warm cuppa when Petra arrived in the dead of night, after a long trip back from Johannesburg.

It was Willow who had carried water and heated it for a warm bath that night or was it morning? It did not matter anymore, because it seemed like it had been eons ago.

If it were not for Peetteri, she would be a real Loner in a strange land. But then she had to admit she was glad to be in Canada rather than alone in South Africa. Petra's life began there and experienced enough trauma for a lifetime. And then to be sent to University in Johannesburg with her father's family as an adult was enough.

Strong of Faith but little of Action that showed the LOVE that the Repentance Grandma Mara constantly preached at her, should bring. Did she not understand how connected Petra was to The InnerNet?

Now Grandad Bokamosa was another story – she sensed they might even be Soulmates. He Listened inwardly too. She could tell by his calm presence amid a Storm. Though at the time, it all seemed so tragic and '*Over the Top*,' so many people's self-righteous opinions being thrown in every direction around her, that made no sense at all to her InnerNet.

Yes, Self-righteous simply means
'Jealousy with a crown' of superiority.

It made her glad again for the Grad Gift someone very gentle and special had given her Graduation Weekend. She knew there were likeminded men who respected a woman and did not take advantage. The Gift of Knowing gave her serious excuse to cut short an Education she did not want, and choose her own path, even though she caused quite a ruckus with Mara Bokamosa.

OR Did Mara cause the ruckus? Looking back now, it was a Wild Ride with Mara, with her Dr. Gardener and the understanding she received of Henri's medication plight as well.

Petra was not aligning with Mara's ideals; though she wondered if Mara was aligned with her own ideals? And now the suspicion that she was 'with child' really upset Mara to have this grandchild living under her roof. And knowing she was spending too much time with undesirable family connections.

A reminder of a child of her own that 'defiled the family'. They were still living that one down because it was so close to home; and her Peter was still supporting the whole bunch of them. Or at least in her own mind he was.

The Bokamosa Grandad had supported Petra in her stay and here they were rewarded with a pregnant grandchild under their care. Even though she did not show, Mara *knew*.

Assumption and Gossip were Mara's Specialties.

Petra thought 'come on, I am 20'. She would have her 21st Birthday on January 17. She had been put back grades in school when she emigrated to Canada. Sara had not. That placed them in the same grade. Sara was brilliant, so they were in different classes and studied different subjects.

The Grandmother informed the Parents the very day of extreme loss. The day, Sara overdosed. Brilliant Sara who escaped home for the Street Life before she finished high school.

And now the parents in a dilemma outside of their *Tidy Lives* were faced with '*another situation*' too devastating for their minds to handle all at once.

Though it probably should have been them, that escaped to 'the Cabin' they decided it was best that Petra go to the Cabin and not return home or even to the City where their compatriots would find out. Finish the term, get the credits, then board a flight back to Canada.

They were in overwhelm. BIG TIME!

How could they have raised 2 Girls to defy their Dreams of a family of Respect they could be proud of? Children to raise their own Social Status above the flaws they created within themselves. How could Petra have conceived when she was on The Pill. They had made sure both girls were being '*Regulated*' by the Pill.

Most of this all made Petra laugh now. She was so glad for Wisdom Willow! So thankful for Willow's LOVE, Wisdom, Healing modalities, and Coaching. Willow, who had delivered Peter. Willow, who reached out to her when she was suddenly alone.

Willow, who stepped in to be a Grandparent to Peetteri when her parents refused to acknowledge Peter or even her.

Pride had disowned her when she needed LOVE the most. When she found LOVE in Grandad and the Gate House folk. Then suddenly ripped from her to honor her parents wishes.

Had they forgotten that she was almost 21? Petra had not yet learned to 'hold her own ground. To Honor her own Integrity above the demands. Petra was still Marching in parental and social Parade Alignment'.

But maybe we missed a piece here, that helps us understand the hidden Truths of so many lives that live behind a Mask of Proud in fear of *'being found out'*.

Chapter 10

During Petra's life with Grandparents, she uncovered a few pieces of history that were secreted away for more than 30 years. Stashed in a file marked "Closed" by Henri. She wondered if Marabella ever knew this one. And maybe one locked away by her mother as well.

Shortly after the term started, a young Professor came to her in the Library. Professor Peter was of mixed race. He taught Mathematics and History of which she had no interest. So, of course, she was in none of his classes.

It started something like this. Petra was pouring over a Book of Ancient Art, unaware of who else was in the Library. She was in 'the Art Zone' so to speak. She heard a male voice, deep like her father's voice and most of the Bokamosa men.

"I apologise for interrupting your studies Miss Karabo-Bokamosa. My name is Peter Bokamosa." He was silent for a few moments to let the information sink into this young lady.

"We share a last name?" replied Petra.

"Yes." Peter responded "and maybe even more than that. I believe the same grandparents on our father's side. I have been doing some family research. If you are interested, I would love to share mine with you, and you can share yours with me."

Bewildered and yet being the curious soul Petra was, she could not resist gaining revelation. "I would be glad to share. It is rather lonely here; living under Mara's strict rule and all." She smiled as he came to sit across the table. Where would this lead?

Peter began. "I have just passed my 30th Birthday. Petra, how old are you?"

Petra said, "On January 17th, I will be 21. I am looking forward to celebrating my 21st Birthday here in the land of my birth."

"Yes, that stands to reason, as I remember some of the family dynamics back then, when you were born, as strangely you did not 'Look' like a Bokamosa. Neither did I."

"My mother is Bob and Naomi's, the Gardeners of earlier years daughter, Maria. My father is Henri Bokamosa. My Grandfather Bob died three years ago. It is a different Gardener now. Mara has had several Gardeners since. None met her liking until this fellow who has been here for over a year.

My mother Maria lived with her parents in the Gate House. I was born when she was just fifteen." Petra gasped!

"Petra, how old is Henri, supposedly your father?"

"Supposedly? my father?"

"Let me see? My parents were both 30 when Sara was born. I know that much. Sara was born 11 months after me. Birthdays and Dates were unimportant in our house."

"Huh! Maybe it is easiest that way if you are hiding facts."

Now where did she ever think that one up? And even express it out loud to Peter. Petra realized that her InnerNet always knew something her parents were not willing to surface. And now she may find out why.

This was not a chance meeting. It was not by chance she was sent back to Africa to study. It was not about becoming a 'Doctor' after all. It was about uncovering her roots, and the reasons behind so many denials and deceptions.

Peter had a similar gentleness to what she experienced in Petri. (Petri a beautiful relationship memory as he was somewhere in the British Isles and she in South Africa, likely to never meet again.) It was easy getting to know Peter. Except that he was several years older than Petri.

This was just the beginning of a relationship unexpected. Where else could a relationship of understanding begin – <u>But in THE LIBRARY</u>. That is where Petri and Petra met as well!

Peter taught no evening classes on Wednesday, so he suggested that they meet after classes that day of the week.

Petra was finished by 3:30. If it were Okay with Petra, could they come to this very table in the Library for an hour of 'Family Dynamics' as they labelled it?

Petra agreed. And that is how it all started. Peter and Petra would invest an hour in History. Peter asked if they could then go for an early Dinner before going to the Gate House as he went there to study the Bible with his Grandmother Naomi and a few others anyway. He sensed she would be interested, so encouraged her to come along if she would like that kind of an evening.

Into the History a few weeks, Petra knew that if she was Henri's child, she was not the oldest after all.

Peter and Petra enjoyed their time together, as well as their discoveries as they dug deeper into the family dynamics. In fact, Petra thought maybe Wednesday was the highlight of her week when going to University in Johannesburg.

Peter told her that Henri and Maria his mother, had a Summer Affair. Of course, there was a huge 'Class Crisis' since she was of different race and color; as well as being from a Gardeners household, whereas The Bokamosa was a wealthy Diamond Mining Empire.

Henri paid Maria more than the usual amount of attention that summer. In a sense, he was bored. He had chosen a summer off from study and work, just so he could relax and restore his mind for the following term that meant he would either succeed as a Medical Student or require an adjustment in educational direction.

Maria had grown and matured into a young woman since Henri had spent anytime looking. She was Beautiful and radiant in an amazing way. Maria was no longer the slightly overweight girl in the backyard.

She was often out in the yard helping her father with the landscape, the planting, the mowing etc. She had a tall slender body with well defined curves. Her skin was a contrast to her white shorts and shirt tied up just below her breasts.

Henri observed from a distance as he sat by the pool and read a book. Or played a flute. Maria heard the flute that stirred her senses. 'Seductive' was the word she used when she told her son the story of his heritage.

When the coast was clear, Henri began inviting Maria for romps in the pool; a privilege that few Gardener's Daughters would get. Her father okayed it, as he saw it as a Liberation where rich and poor; black and white could mix freely. Where maybe the wealthy Family he worked for, which he had to admit paid him a good living, had 'laid down the hatchet to pick up the flute' so to speak.

Maria was interested in hearing Henri's perspective on life, university, and a lot of other things she may never have privilege of.

It was not long before lust and passion brought them even closer together. A month into summer, and Henri began inviting Maria into more than the pool. She was curious as to what Wealthy Folks had in their homes, so she was keen on the invitation. Henri fixed them a cool drink. A taste that Maria had never tasted before – Expensive Wine!

Maria became very mellow and mouldable under that influence and especially when Henri began playing the flute. He had a very seductive way about the notes he chose. She admired how powerful music could be. That is when Henri would start to gently caress and kiss those full lips. Powerful and overwhelming the arousal for a young woman.

Noticed by someone with Wealth. Noticed by a man soon to become a Doctor.

Maria knew 'this is what Love Stories are made of'. Never once did it occur to her that she could be being 'taken advantage of'. That this could be a Game he had played more than once. Henri knew the rules of the game.

Maria did not.

Gently, so gently and subtill. No rushing her. No pressure. Just that seductive Flute. That mellow cocktail in the afternoon when it was too hot to be in the pool.

Henri suggested to his parents that they hire Maria to do some cleaning everyday. She could be the one to change the sheets twice a week. It would relieve his mother, who spent a lot of time in the office at the mine during that time after children were grown.

And so, Maria became a constant attendant at Henri's side. No, he was not lazy, because he was home all day, he was required to keep up the laundry and ready the evening meal etc.

He found that Maria was an incredibly good cook. Henri and Maria would design a meal that they would create together for the family when they arrived after work. They were not a big family. David his brother was working at the mine with his parents Mara and Peter Sr.

Of course, if Maria got to stay at all, it was as a server and to clean up the kitchen. Peter was sure that Grandad Peter would have loved to have Maria at the table too, but Mara was very 'Upper Class' and had the say at the house.

Summer went well and enjoyable. However, as it got closer to university starting again, the caressing and exploration became greater – especially when it was Maria's duty to change beds twice a week. She liked clean sheets too – but twice in a week?

Now that is Luxury!

One day Henri came in while she was changing the sheets in his room. He came out from the bathroom unexpected when she thought he was out doing his daily run. She usually tried to do his Sheet Change early in the day when he was out running.

This day surprised her. Startled, she whirled around to see he only had briefs on. Well, that should not be much different than his speedos in the pool. For some reason Maria became extremely uncomfortable being in this room at this time, with this man. It was that weird look in his eyes that she had never seen before.

She wished a thousand times over, that she had put more layers of clothing on that morning. She was not sure why, but she sensed her life and admiration for Henri suddenly evaporate.

In a flash, he had her pinned to the bed, stripping her of the little she did have on. She could not believe what was happening to her. This was not the gentle Henri of the past couple of months. This was a crazed demon possessed with lust and taking what he wanted without any regard for her feelings or pleasure.

Her arms were pinned behind her back stripped of her skirt and panties and her legs spread over the end of the bed, he was forcibly entering and thrusting. How could he do this to her?

Why was he doing this to her?

Why could she not so much as scream or even reason with him?

She felt the thrusting increasing and wanted to Scream NO! NO! but no sound escaped. She was holding her breath. Unmercifully he thrust and thrust and thrust while holding her pulling and pulling at her nipples.

How cruel!

How mean!

Why was this happening to her anyway?

Finally, he exhausted what he had to give. And with a hideous laugh said, 'I don't take without giving back'. She could not move, because somehow her hands were behind her back still.

How could he do this to her? Holding her hands with one of his, the other still pulling at a nipple, he ducked down to the foot and spread her legs again. Was he going to inject again?

Oh! please don't her body was yelling, even though she could not voice anything. Her mouth was so dry.

Just then he began to suck and suck, where he had just exited.

This was her pay? What did he mean?

Her body now seemed to take on a life of its own. First it was a tingle, then it was more forcefully moving and convulsing. She somehow got a hand loose and tried to push his head up and off where he was sucking. He only chuckled and sucked harder.

Exhausted she passed out. Her mind, her emotions, her nervous system spent.

When she awakened, her clothes were back on, and she was laying on the sofa in the great room. Had it all been a Nightmarish dream? She heard no one in the house. She tiptoed down the hall to see that the beds were all made. The muscles by her crotch hurt. Henri was gone.

The family would soon be home.

So, Maria took herself home quietly and unobserved. She found the silence of her own room to understand what had just happened. Her parents were away for a couple of days. This to her advantage to think, to pray things through, yet fearful she would be found alone.

Why had he raped her in such a frenzied way? Why could it not have happened during the gentle times of being remarkably close and in the others embrace?

Why did he not ask her for permission? Had he been gentle in the asking, and the bed being so convenient, she would likely have melted under his touches.

But this?

This hideous memory?

How strange life is.

What was she going to tell her folks? Did she need to report this? Would she get her family into deep trouble and they would not have a job – no money, no home? Finally, she decided to just keep quiet. It would be her word against his and she knew she did not stand a chance.

He after all 'WAS THE KING'S SON'! She told no one.

After missing 4 periods, and gaining weight, she asked her mother what it felt like to be pregnant?

Her mother's mouth dropped. She came and folded Maria in her embrace. "Honey, I knew something happened. I have been trying to figure it out. You have been incredibly quiet, not your bubbly self."

"Did he Do It to you? Was it something you consented to?"

Maria burst out in tears. She sobbed and sobbed as her mother, Naomi, quietly held her and without judgement held space for Maria. Eventually, Maria could sob no more. She was spent.

And then in a low voice said, "had he seduced me gently when he played the flute and gave me wine, it could have been a beautiful thing, and yes, I likely would have consented."

"But this, but this – Mom he had a demon I swear. Oh, what oh what is within me? Do you think the one within me is a demon, Mom?"

"Honey, it is something we will just have to ride through together. I am here for you all the way. I will make sure Bokamosa pays for your care, and for the care of the child."

"I Know too many of their secrets. They give me what I ask to keep their name 'unspotted'."

"I do not gossip. They all know they can Trust my wisdom."

Chapter 11

"And Petra, that is my Mother's story!"

"Perhaps that is my Story as well. I am thankful for my grandmother, Naomi, who interceded on my mother's behalf. We were well supplied for. However, we were never accepted either. In some families it seems they cannot see beyond their money. They take advantage wherever they can and whenever."

"Petra, I need to clarify that. Grandad Peter, who I am named after, is not like the rest. He is a Diamond among a lot of wasted rock."

Petra, I believe we should send for your DNA analysis. As you said, you do not know if Henri is your birthright or not. I am of the impression he is not.

My grandma was every ones confident. Like she often said 'if I were to write a book, it would be a best seller. I have so many stories inside of me'. Of course, she never did."

"We lived with my grandparents in the Gate House until I was finished university."

"I remember your mother Marabella very well. She would often sneak off to the Gate House for a visit with Grandma Naomi when they came out to visit. One day after you were born, she brought you over with her. I got to touch your tiny hands, but then was sent out. Yes, I went out of the room, but listened through the wall.

– you know when you put a hollow tube to the wall or a glass and can hear very well. That is what this 9-year-old did. Gram would never tell, but I heard. Marabella told Gram that Henri was not your father, because you looked so much like the guy from America that she dated during university."

"They had their final farewell the night before your Mom moved to Johannesburg and he went back to America. Seems he belonged to a native American Tribe. I believe she said too, but I had forgotten until I see you now."

Petra asked, "do you know what his name is? I found some photos of Mom and a young man in a biology book in the attic. I wonder if it was him? I do resemble him some. On the back of the photo was written 'Love you ALWAYS, Ben Parker."

"Peter, thank you for all you have done for me. What would I have done these months if it were not for our visits? I so look forward to Wednesdays with you. You have been good to me for sure."

And then she added "It is likely best that we are not siblings or half siblings. Yes, you would be a half sibling to Sara, but not to me. However, we best wait until the DNA results come back. I can hardly wait!"

"I am excited about coming clean and knowing who we are. All the deceptions frustrate me. All the lies! How can people live with themselves hiding behind a mask of what they think they should be to others?"

"Exactly! I have often thought that myself. I know as a little boy, I longed for a father figure – someone to be ruff with, someone to read to me or watch the games I played at school. Grampa was good, but he was old too. Henri never once even took notice of me. Maybe that is wrong – he could not help but notice I existed. But he seemed to avoid me, avoid the Gate house and anything else to do with my mom.

So, it is exceptional that Marabella often came over to visit my grandmother when you all lived nearby, before going to Canada. I have wondered if the move to Canada removed him from the guilt over what he did to my mother; and me bringing a constant reminder of his error?"

"Peter Sr. was good to me as well. I am just getting a flashback of a day Grandad took you and I out to the mine. You stood between my knees to be tall enough to see out the window of the truck. I think you must have been about 6 and very curious – full of questions about the Sparkling Stones."

"Anyway, I am glad my Mother had family support. Many do not. Because of growing up like I did, I vowed I would never take advantage without a strong commitment on both sides to be 'A Family' fully participating. And here I am 30 years old, and without an attachment."

"Petra, you are the easiest person I have found to be with that is anywhere near my age. You do my heart good too. It is a good thing you are not in my classes."

"Why is that Peter?"

"Well, I feel like my heart is being won by your gentle, non-judgemental spirit and I would be distracted."

"Peter, I like the poet RUMI. This is my version of something he said several hundred years ago:

"Before attitudes, critical analysis, judgements, and opinions, there is a Garden of LOVE.

I will meet you there.

"That is where Capital LOVE sees everything. That is the space I like to visit in. From what you have related to me, I like your grandma Naomi. That is where she meets people too."

"I suppose we should be getting back to The Bokamosa Estate before I turn into something I should not in Mara's eyes." They both laughed and got up from the table.

Chapter 12

Petra had not been feeling the best. She thought she might have a touch of a flu. However, she was Emotional too. Foods she was not used to; intensity of studies and missing Petri though she did not want to think about heartache/heartbreak.

It was her fault as much as his that they had not thought to follow up on continued communication. Perhaps they were simply giving the other Space to Grow. If they were meant to be as One, some day they would meet again.

But where and how? She was beginning to feel like she would stay in South Africa after all; and likely he would end up in the USA or who knows where. For now, being with Peter and the Gate House family filled the LOVE gap for her.

Mara Bokamosa knew all the right/wrong questions to ask and assume. She found out Petra was visiting a lot with Peter, and it was not in the least of her liking.

"This smartie Pete who thought he was *so great as a university professor* when he was an illegitimate of the gardener's daughter. Such a dirty girl anyway. Flaunting herself before men!

She saw no reason why her family felt obligated to support such low downs. And to think that Henri thought she should hire her for household chores!" Mara was in complete denial that her precious son might have some responsibility in the obligation.

"And then poor Henri gets stuck with this Marabella freeloader – obviously, she was pregnant before he met her. Married so fast! No wonder Henri is a basket case and on medication to keep his nerves calm!"

If she had her way, none of this would have happened. This young lady that is not pleasing her, would not even be here. Afterall, she looks more like those emigrants from India/Asia that work the coffee fields.

PETRA IS NOT OURS!

PETER IS NOT OURS!

She would like to have given a Primal Scream for all the misfortunate relationships in the Bokamosa Estate; but, of course, her righteous soul must endure all this stuff outside of her control.

But she was thankful her Peter let her do pretty much her own liking and choosing for the gardens and house. She was impressed with Dr. Gardener and what he was doing for the Roses. How could she be so lucky in finding him. It was satisfying that she had someone to be with that understood her needs as a woman as well.

Oh yes! There was a lot she controlled – a lot that she covered butt for others about. Thankful she had the decency to be an Upstanding Member of The Church and Horticultural Society.

And now, this Petra and Peter must be playing the fool again – lusting in fleshly things. She did not want this child (well she is a woman old enough to choose for herself) in her house, especially knowing who she was spending way too much time with.

Mara would see to it that she was sent back to Canada as soon as was possible, whether she wanted to or not. She would not have a Peter and Petra marriage on her hands.

What confusion of relations that would be?

It is enough that there is someone among her kin that is 'his own grandpa' kind of forced upon her of course. What a mix up of marriages! How could an old man father his son's child?

Anyway, she did not even want to think about it. To many memories surfacing. Why was this Petra doing this to her?

At least she and Peter kept their vows now for over 50 years. Considering Peter was always at the mine and spent little time at home, too tired for much more than work, it is a wonder they even had 3 children.

Of course, it was her choice to not have more. All the pain and ridiculous weight gains she worked so hard to get rid of once every child was born. All born before she was even twenty years old.

Did Peter care?

Certainly, he did not make any comments about her hard work to stay fit. But then Peter was a 'doer' and not a 'talker'.

His father at least could make a woman feel good with his comments. Maybe part of why she kept in as good a shape as she did after his kids. She liked his admiration, even though she knew this was not the wisest relationship.

But then it is easy to keep in shape before you are 20. After that, the body has a mind of its own. David has been dead for 40 years now. She missed him in the house. Her mother-in-law had died just after David jr. was born. And now even her David was gone for more than 10 years.

At least Professor Gardener noticed and knew what a woman likes to hear. She told herself smugly as if to complement herself on finding such an interesting Gardener.

By the end of November Mara decided she had enough – seeing these two, Peter and Petra, go off on weekends together was more than she could endure.

Of course, she was not jealous. The possibilities were what simply irritated her.

She sent a text off to Henri to let him know what she _assumed_ was going on in South Africa. Give them time to make plans to get Petra out of her way before the New Years Party.

She wanted her house to herself now that she no longer went to the office most days. It was enough that her Peter would be in the Estate House more after the end of the year.

See, and there we go again – Two Peters living on the same land for twenty-four years! At least 'My Peter's' father was David and not another Peter.

Yes, she had named her first child after his father David. But having David times two was different than having two Peters if you know what I mean; she consoled herself with an old memory, smiling at the feeling of it.

Why did that Maria girl have to name her son after my Peter? OR? Was it that tight lipped Naomi that suggested it?

"That tight lipped Naomi!" she said to no one in particular, for she was talking with herself.

Mara knew she knew a lot of things that she, herself would like to know, but Naomi told no one anything.

She never spoke a word unkind about anyone, though she knew a lot about everyone. A lot of people dumped on Naomi. She had herself and was glad she had someone to talk to way back when she was but a teen. 'Just think – married at 14!

Unimaginable! But 50 years have past and more by now.'

Though she admitted to herself that she was glad for Naomi's secrecy when it came to her own story. Only Naomi knew now that David Bokamosa was dead.

So, though she would love to know what people told Naomi about their lives, she was very thankful that Naomi kept her mouth shut about what she knew about 'Mara'. But that is another story.

Right now, she needed her house to herself. With this girl here, she did not feel free lest she come home unexpected during the day; or even be sick enough to stay home all day.

Oh my! What a plight she was in.

So off she went for her cell phone to text Henri the goings on of Johannesburg, South Africa; in particular, the Bokamosa Estate.

Chapter 13

Within ten days, the DNA results were back. Peter waited until they were together to open the package. He was glad he had access to the Lab because of his History Classes.

Both excited by the possibilities the package held, Peter and Petra decided to leave the Library and go to a park to be by themselves.

Peter had a beach cover in his vehicle, so they found a secluded area and spread it out. Peter let Petra open the package and spill the contents on the mat between them.

The package, among other things made suggestion as to possible parentage and nationality connections. It would only be those connections that had also gotten their DNA sampled that were in the Data Base.

Petra knew that Henri had both his and hers done at a point her mother did not know about. Of course, being young, she did not have access to those results. She wondered if there were more names in there now, more possibilities? At that time, he said it was a Science Project.

His, not hers, of course.

As they sat side by side now, and poured over the names and information, Petra found out she could descend from The Sioux Nation, which inhabited the mid USA and Canada – North Dakota, South Dakota, Northern Minnesota, Southern Saskatchewan, and Manitoba.

She also had a tiny bit of the Asian/India DNA.

It was not long before they spotted Marabella's Dutch/British connection and her name as a possible parent as well.

They now knew that *Dad's Science Project* may have included all Four of them at that time.

Interesting!

Petra wondered out loud 'I wonder if Dad shared the results with Mom or was it all tucked neatly in a file folder in a file cabinet in his office like a lot of other things he kept under lock and key?

Down the list they scan. What? There is that 'Benjamin Patrick Parker'. They both spotted it at the same time and laughed together. Soulmates!

Petra wondered where the Asia/Indian may have come in? She may have to search for her mother's read out once she was home. Or – no, it would not come from Henri. It would have to be something in Marabella's heritage.

Immediately, they were curious about 'Benjamin Patrick Parker'. Where was he now? Was he still a Doctor? And Where? What Hospital or University did he work out of? Or was he a Doctor? Maybe he was a tourist that met Marabella.

Twenty-one years would have passed since he and Marabella likely had contact. Excitement gave rise to a lot of speculation.

Peter had brought his MacBook, so he punched in <u>Benjamin Parker</u>. There were 5 to choose from. – a doctor at the Mayo Hospital in Rochester, MN

- A truck driver living in Dallas, TX.
- A Property Management Consultant in Winnipeg, MB
- A pilot with Alaskan Air
- And yet again a professor in Cape Town, South Africa
- And a person owning a property on Vancouver Island, BC but an Irish citizen

"Oh! Now how close can that be to home?"

Anyway, they agreed that anyone of these could be one and the same. Likely it was the professor in Cape Town, since Marabella had gone to Med School there.

The Property Manager that lived in Canada that had the property on Vancouver Island was way to close to home.

All through their Dining and Evening they drew up all kinds of scenarios as to how Petra might find her Birth Father. Maria had joined them for Dinner this evening, and they were all excited to share their findings with her.

She worked at the Sports Club not far from their favorite diner.
In the end, there was nothing conclusive, and they expressed the fun it had been to view the possibilities and plan next steps.

Peter was becoming more and more excited to plan a Holiday to Canada and Explore – Follow up on some of the possibilities.

Never once did it occur to them that this Ben Parker may not be as happy as they to meet. Sometimes that happens when children are adopted. One ex-parent might accept them back in their lives; while another 'Closed the File' years before and hoped no one would snoop.

Petra tucked the package into her backpack just before Peter dropped her off.

That was not the end of Petra's searching through the archives on the computer that night. The Cape Town Prof or the Minnesota Doctor were likely the closest possibilities in Petra's mind, assuming her father would likely be in a medical field since Marabella was. But then again, maybe not.

Sleep evaded her.

Morning came way too soon.

Chapter 14

The next few weeks flew by so quickly. Petra was beginning to really settle in and enjoy her time in Johannesburg. Peter and Petra spent a lot more time together exploring more that DNA Documents and Family History.

A few weekends, Peter took Petra to more distant places to get a sense of what South Africa was really like. One weekend they went on a Safari that included Maria.

By this time in history, there was not as much tension as when Henri and Marabella moved to Canada. Since both were of mixed races, it really was not strange to see them together.

It was only Grandma Mara that complained about their being together and it not being a good idea. It was not so bad when Grandad Peter was home. Petra felt welcome in his presence. He told her a lot about his history and the Mining Industry. He told her how a Diamond is cut and shaped.

Mara's nose would snort in the air and go about serving as if she could not tolerate the fact of hearing more mine data. Or was it that she had to share 'my Peter' with someone else?

One Saturday, Peter sr. invited both Petra and Peter to come along with him to the mine. He explained the steps and the value of the pieces he showed them.

Finally, he gave Petra a tiny uncut stone. "Petra, you are like this uncut stone. Each experience of life will cut a facet to reflect a new light. The more experiences the more the facet cuts, the more your Light will Dazzle your Beholder."

"It is obvious you have experiences already, more than a lot, because you already radiate. I do not require an answer Petra, but I noticed your mood switch last week. Maybe the 'grinder dust' in your eyes. I understand."

"I can also see that Mara is using a harsh grinder while you are with us. It is bringing an unexpected shine out in you. When I paid your ticket to come, I was hoping she would love having grandchildren here too. Sadly, for both of us she does not."

He swallowed and looked Peter's way. "I think this Peter", he affectionately poked Peter, "is using a softer brush with you." He chuckled. It would do his heart good for these two to decide they have a 'LOVE affair' and settle down right here close to him.

Imagine Great-Grandchildren almost next door. Of course, he would not be meddling in any way. There was enough of that with one person on the Estate being meddling too often.

"Has Peter told you that he is Henri's son – my name sake?" The smile and gentleness between them spoke loudly to Petra. Two Peters Loving as the Creator created humans to LOVE.

"But, Petra, that does not make you his half sister. Your sister Sara is. They are both Henri's prodigy."

"Now here may come the hard part Petra, I do not believe you are Henri's child. In saying this, please understand that I still love you as my Granddaughter just as much as the rest."

"I love your Marabella too. Henri has a nature like Mara. I understand what your Marabella puts up with. I admire her for staying with him all these years too. She inspires me to stick with it."

"I do my humble best to live LOVE with no duality. Young ones' we either move closer into the Eternal LOVE Circle or we move away from LOVE – I am talking Creator LOVE, Eternal LOVE that Rejoices the Soul.

You may not see me going to Church with Mara, but I have a deep Connection to my Creator. Naomi taught me how."

Petra ventured to say "Grandad, I have noticed that. I call this <u>my InnerNet Connection</u>."

"Child, that is a perfect analogy. I must remember that term. <u>InnerNet</u>"

"You ever thought of being a Life Coach? I think you would be a good one. You are not cut out to be a doctor in your parent's practice. You are too Connected and would have a hard time fitting into all that chemistry stuff. You are more like me – Connected to the Elements and Creator."

He continued "This getting you back here to Johannesburg for *some Education*, was a request on my part. Strange as it may seem, I wanted to give you some information firsthand."

"I wanted to get you acquainted with the Diamond Industry, and the analogies I have learned. When you were small, you were often my shadow and visited here at the mine."

"It bothered me that Mara was so not in LOVE with this precious little critter that asked a ton of questions beyond what she could understand."

"Awe! Grandad, that is why deep within me I know things about Diamonds! I often stop by the jewelry counter when I am in a mall to look for a diamond that really grabs my attention. And most of the ones I pick up are 'Bokamosa' Diamonds. Of course, I am not in possession of any yet. It is on my 'Wish List' when my income starts coming of my own earning, I will get a Bokamosa Diamond something."

"Petra, what does the Bokamosa Diamond something look like in your mind" asked Grandad?

It did not take much to bring up the image in mind. "Grandad, it is a Gold Ring with 3 small Diamonds set in. Not out so they might get knocked off but set in the gold. I know it will be expensive, but I will save for it. And no, I have not seen it in a display counter yet."

Grandad smiled very mischievously. "Okay. Now we best get back to this Parentage thing I brought you back here for and specifically brought you here today to explain. I know that few people know the truth of the matter, but it matters to me deeply."

"There is a wise woman who tells no-one anything that anyone ever tells her. However, I also have an Inside Track." He winked at the younger Peter.

"From the research I have done – I am quite sure your birth father is a man by the name of Ben Parker. A Dr. Benjamin Parker. My research indicates that he was a professor at the university in Cape Town when Marabella was training. I do know he was a good friend of your mother before she met Mara's Henri."

Young Peter and Petra, now sitting in Grandad's office winked at each other with a smile of enjoyment when grandad looked away gathering his thoughts. He may already know without them having to do a lot more research.

"This Dr. Parker presently lives in Rochester, MN USA and practices at the Mayo Clinic. You know the World-Famous Hospital Clinic that a couple of Doctor brother's started on donations.

To me, that gives a lot of credential to a place. Not being paid by some chemical company to indoctrinate students to use their drugs."

Senior Peter continued "A few years ago, I had a medical problem that nothing here seemed to resolve. Mara only knows that I went somewhere for treatments. But that is where I went."

"One of the Doctors, and there were many, was Dr. Benjamin Parker. We spent some time in an evening comparing notes and sharing his time and impressions of South Africa. Of course, he was as far as east is from west in South Africa away."

"I enjoyed the fellow. When he found out I was from Johannesburg, he wondered if I had ever heard of a Dr. Karabo, Dr. Marabella Karabo?"

"I said Sure have. It is a small world after all. You know what? My son, Henri, married her. He was all ears to hear where they were and how they were and a lot of other stuff."

"The man looked to be of an American Native Tribe. He invited me to his home one evening and showed me photo and told me about his family history as well. Seems he was not married either. Guess he liked it better that way. Doesn't have to hang out at the hospital to keep peace in the house like I hung out at the mine." He winked at Peter "and hang out at Naomi's now."

Both listeners caught that one instantaneously. "Now we know Grandad – you hang out here so Grandmother Mara can do what she wants at home with the Professor Gardner."

And Petra added "I feel like she thinks I am in the way; so, that is part of the reason I asked to move to the Gate House. Peter's grandmother seems to enjoy the visits too."

"She is a good one, Petra. She holds a lot of secrets she *ain't tellin'* nobody!"

"So back to our history lesson - That is when I got up front and personal. I outright asked him.

'Did you and Marabella sleep together before she left Cape Town?'

He blushed and said, 'Why would you ask?'

I says well I have a granddaughter that *do not* look nothing like Henri. She does look a lot like you."

"It took him a silent minute to let it register. I just remained quiet because I know it might be a jolt to a fella to find out he has a child he never knew about. Especially when that child is maybe fifteen."

"Next day, when I returned to the hospital for my treatment, the man thanked me for bringing it to his attention. He said he sent for a DNA test, so that if ever my granddaughter sent for hers, there might be a match up."

"A nice kind of man."

"So, Petra, that is why I brought you both out here today. I will pay to have a DNA test if you so desire. If it is a match, I have something for you."

Petra took a deep breath. "Grandad, this is all remarkably interesting and confirming. To be honest, Peter and I have been discussing this very topic. Peter paid to have it done. Last week the results came back."

She looked pensive at Peter and took a deep breath to continue.

"I am going to expose Peter now as well as my own snoopiness. Before we left here, I often went to the attic and snooped through the books and photos. I was about Eight. Two photos fell out of a Biology Text. The man looked like me, or I looked like him more exact; so, I stole the photo away to my Bible, where I felt like no one would discover I had taken it. On the back it says,

"Love you Always,
Ben Parker."

"I am sure it was my mothers. All those books were boxed away and left behind when we left for Canada. To confirm the Ben Parker, when Peter was little, and I was born, Peter told me he touched my little hands when Marabella took me over to the Gate House without Mara noticing. Peter was not allowed to be where they started visiting, but he listened through the wall. He told me he believed my father was a Ben Parker from America."

"How fascinating this all is!"

"Actually, Grandad, I have the document right here in my pack." Petra opened her backpack and presented Senior Peter with the document. He smiled without opening it and pulled out a package from his desk drawer. Handed it to Petra.

"This Petra is not from me, but from your very own Daddy."

It was a large brown business envelop. It was not addressed to Petra.

It was addressed to Jamie Gillette.

The letter read:

Dear Jamie,

Somehow, I have always known you existed. Our Sioux Nation has a legend that when we truly listen, the Great Spirit tells us things we do not know or remember we know. I did not know who you were, or who might bring you back to me again, but I did know my Jamie is somewhere.

You have an incredibly special Grandfather. I am sad because injury brought our paths together. But I am super grateful the Spirit gave us a meeting place on neutral ground.

I will not interfere with your life or your mother's. Perhaps she still holds a secret that she does not wish to disclose. Some people live life thinking that way. I on the other hand choose Transparency.

What was I to answer when your Grandfather abruptly asked a searching question? The answer is yes. By now, you have matched DNA and know for yourself.

One little piece of advice, Dear One: "With Christ, (Eternal LOVE) Be the Love you are looking for. Accept no man's proposal in marriage, until the one comes who he <u>himself</u> is 'the Love <u>he is</u> looking for'.

This love is not in love with oneself, for that may be Narcissistic and tragic.

This is a LOVE that holds humility and embraces the under-standing that: "With Christ we are enough." (Christ is Creator's Perfect Expression of Eternal Love)

I trust that I may be the Grandfather of your children.

I look forward to the day of our meet up.

Love you Always,

Ben Parker

Petra folded the paper back into the envelope and took the box.

As she opened, the green velvet box, Petra saw the most exquisite Diamond Ring. Not a large diamond, but three small and perfectly cut

Diamonds. A Diamond representing the three people involved - Ben, Marabella and his Jamie.

The sparkle of the Diamonds reflected in Petra's smile. "Grampa this is exquisite. Is this from you?"

"Look inside the ring Petra".

Petra turned the ring to catch the light. There engraved was 'To my beloved Jamie, BPP'.

"Grandad is this from your Diamonds?"

"Yes, but I cannot take credit for the cutting or the setting. I am a ruff man. It takes someone perfectly accurate to cut a diamond. The more facets there are, the more expensive the diamond. You have 3 expensive diamonds set in this Gold Ring, ordered by your Birth Father."

"He may not have been there to raise you, but he is waiting for your contact when you are ready for a meeting. Take your time and give it a lot of thought. This is not just about you Jamie."

(she quietly noted Grandad had shifted her name too)

"You have a set of parents that could be offended should he come into your picture too soon. Yes, it is about you, but it is also about the fragility of their relationship. Just as for Marabella not knowing about Peter here, Henri likely has never been told about Ben Parker and his part in your conception."

"It is good when people can be upfront with their partner, but in many cases, it is used as an Atomic Bomb when rough times come."

"I trust your judgement. You are a wise woman with wisdom beyond your years. I now know why. Benjamin Parker is an incredibly wise and intelligent man."

Chapter 15

Petra was thankful for the move to the Gate House. Still, she knew she must indulge Mara for the evening meal. Grandad's presence made it easy.

She knew deep within, that Mara was scheming something, but she did not know what. Though she knew that Mara would love to know about the ring, she said nothing. She knew Grandad would not have informed her either. It was like their hidden secret, their joke on Mara.

Some evenings, when Peter and Petra were at the Gate House, Grandad would stop and visit too. Grandmother Naomi lived by herself now. Peter's grandfather died three years prior to Petra's return to South Africa.

Petra believed that Naomi was likely Grandad's Soulmate, though she was sure it was non-sexual. Maybe they had been Soulmates for decades – the reason he smiled at Peter when he had said 'he had an inside track'.

Senior Peter and Naomi certainly complemented each other. They needed the other to converse with: like it had been with herself and Petri before she left for Africa and he for England.

Someone to understand without judgement. Someone to touch without demand. Someone to simply BE quiet with.

They all knew that Mara had her own stream of visitors in a week; probably why Petra was in her way.

As curious as Mara was about The Ring, she knew that somehow, she would weasel the giver thereof out of Petra within a week.

Petra was just as aware that Mara knew how to control 'passive aggressively' and she would keep her secret along with Grandad. In fact, Mara was sure she knew the giver.

Both Peters and Petra knew she thought she had the answer to their 'Secret' and were leading her question on in her own direction. However, they could never have guessed how Mara would bring Petra's stay at the Estate to an end. There were surprises waiting for everyone. Possibly no one knew. Not even the selfish mind that was arranging their immediate future.

A Narcissistic Attitude does not recognize itself and still manipulates everyone in the direction of its own selfish desire.

Petra had experienced that in being raised under Henri's roof. She really did admire her mom for all the years she tolerated his need for the attention and the control. Petra was glad for her mother's ability to let a lot of it slide off just like water on a duck's back.

How could they not see that they caused a lot of Emotional Suffering in others? No wonder Grandad had the illness he had and went to another Continent for healing! Petra felt like she would have too.

And now, she wondered that even though Grandad said he pushed for her return to Africa, how much of it was Mara's to force Grandad to see that Petra was not theirs?

Whatever the reasonings, Petra was fond of Grandad Peter, and was more than happy that she had these months to get to know him now that she was an adult.

A Kindred Spirit recognizes a Kindred Spirit. Soulmates of LOVE that radiate the LIGHT.

Those who choose to live in darkness do their best to extinguish the Light, often to their own unexpected hurt, tripping over their own disconnection as their darkness blinds them.

No one's feelings matter but their own. No responsibility is taken for the feelings of others. The hurt can always be *Shamed* on someone else, which seems to make them momentarily happy.

"See I told you I was right" is the Essence their life shows while all the while craving more and more 'blame to shame others with.'

And so, Naomi, Petra and the Two Peters kept The Ring Secret while giving Mara what she wanted - GOSSIP!

Mara's Story - The Engagement Ring between Peter and Petra. She knew their behavior was less than honorable. And here she was an accomplice in their crime. She would not have it so.

Would they be Married abruptly before she could have any say? *Illegitimate Children hidden in the guise of Holy Matrimony?*

Would they be married as quickly as her Henri? Oh, how she felt for that boy – having to raise someone else's child? And with that flippant Marabella that never looks at anything seriously.

Heavens! She did not even get to meet the girl until Henri had a ring around her finger. And it was no Bokamosa Diamond, that one. What was he thinking anyway?

Henri was always her favorite because she could say 'Henri is All Bokamosa.' She wondered if she could say that of David; but she was never going to expose anyone's birthright, especially when it meant she had a home, wealth and her children would have an Inheritance extraordinary.

Though by now, David had died in a street fight; and Mayana had died of leukemia as a preteen. Henri's Sara was her only grandchild. She would continue to live with a *'weak man'* that never argued or challenged her on anything.

Now, she might have been a Street Child, but she was A Strong Woman; with the help of David Bokamosa Sr., of course.

That was beside the point!

She had worked with Peter for years. She deserved all the perks she had now. She did not deserve to have another generation living under her roof.

Chapter 16

Henri and Marabella – Both girls had been gone now, for over 2 months. Sara for nearly 2 years. It was a relief to settle into what being a couple is like. They had been pretty much bound to family since Day 1.

They decided on a 5-year plan, which would include selling the Cabin; selling their Practice; selling their home, and maybe even the motorhome. It would be lovely to be debt-free. To the point of being free to spend and invest the money, instead of being 'Debt Propelled'.

Lots of major expenditures - Henri's way of feeling important about his success. Marabella, on the other hand saw each one as more work; more responsibility, and more dollars to keep up.

If Henri carried out his part, took responsibility for the payments and upkeep, it would be easier. He would buy, and then expect her to keep the books straight and the 'ends meeting'. He liked the having thereof, but not the paying, therefore.

Marabella had the suspicion that he grew up that way. Here is the Credit Card; we will look after the paying thereof. Money was always available for most anything he wished for without having to earn his own in life. The few short years she lived in Johannesburg she saw that in his mother.

Marabella was happy just putting in her shifts on the Prenatal Ward at the Hospital. That was enough along with raising daughters and house upkeep.

Henri insisted they needed A Clinic downtown as well. A place for a constant flow of patients who were not hospitalized. A place for examinations and prescriptions etc. It also meant having a Receptionist and at least one Nurse Aid to assist in the rooms. But then again, Henri was from a Family of Wealth. Marabella was not.

Marabella was just grateful for Scholarships that assisted her through medical school. Also, grateful that there were a couple of Profs at the University that raised her cause, that assisted her in ways she never dreamed possible on her own. When she started, she knew it was 'Who you knew, not only What you knew' that got you beyond a certain level in medical. Fortunately, she had both working for her.

Yes, her parents were Societal Rebels. Children of Wealthy parentage that rebelled against Wealth and chose an 'easy go lucky' approach to living. They traveled a lot, to the learning advantage of their children. They had fixed up an old school bus to live and travel in. After 4 kids, it was tight quarters. Fortunate for them, that the weather permitted a lot of outside living.

They were the Artsy Creative Type that managed to sell enough of their work and to get Commissioned work to live well. Dad was author to several books on raising children 'From Scratch'. She was sure the Lifestyle they lived, was his 'Scientific Scratch Experiment' proving it worked before he wrote about it.

Though neither had a university education, they often had gigs at Universities and other Lifestyle Events as Lecturers. Marabella, never quite knew how the income came in, though she was never hungry or without love. Still, Marabella saw that she wanted Freedom to do her own Lifestyle choosing.

Her mother's parents were often her refuge. They had a special pad behind the trees where the Bus could park and have Electrical Connection. Parked exactly right, as Dad was incredibly good at, the Bus opened onto a covered deck with lots of Solar Lighting.

Grandfather Karabo was a GP. It was his influence that led the brilliant Marabella into the medical field. Between Grandparent funding, and scholarships, Marabella had little debt when she finished University and got the position in Johannesburg.

She deliberately applied to Hospitals far from where she was raised. She chose her own Liberation. Previous Files marked 'Closed' whether completely dealt with or not.

She appreciated Family, but she did not see that she needed to be bound to them and their rules. Perhaps her own parents gave her that vision from their own lack of rules. Dad claimed children did not need Rules if they were taught how to choose for themselves.

However, it was not Marabella's plan to be married with family the first year of Practice. It was not in her plan to marry an emotionally crippled man. She grew up with, and previously dated, Strong Gentlemen.

No, she did not recognize Henri's disability for several months. They were both so busy getting oriented into the Medical Practice, topped off by the birth of a Beautiful Daughter – and then just as quickly, another.

Henri had displayed the Best of the Best when they met and started out together. She guessed now that Love can hide a multitude of deception for quite a long time. She also saw that she kept the blinders on for a long time too.

Now do not get me wrong. Henri is a good man. He is a good doctor; it is just that he has 'His Moments'. A Heckle and Hyde personality.

The first she learned was to watchout for the New Moon stage. They often joked about their 'Regulars' - same people with the same issues every New Moon at the Emergency. She poked at him 'that he might be one of them'. He took the poke calmly. He heard it loud and clear; and yet he had no idea how to correct his own mental wellness.

Yes, he met her poke with one of his own when it was PMS time. And then to think that he would have to put up with THREE women in the house eventually, all cycling at the same time. *He might have to take the days off and go Fishing or something.*

After moving to Canada, and the pressure of life and Status Quo being even greater, Henri started consulting with a Psychiatrist. Of course, the accepted strategy was mood modifiers or suppressors.

It was not the first time in Henri's life that pharmaceuticals were called into action. Each time they required changing, the depression and pressure in his head got worst for a few days before the miraculous happened and he could easily handle the workload again.

During this time, he often found something more to buy. Marabella suspected that '*The Shopping Therapy*' was of more value than the new prescription.

She also saw that their intimate interactions took on a bizarre twist. Oh yes, she tolerated the extremes, but questioned them in her own mind. Usually, it was her that was left exhausted.
Sometimes she would sleep with one of the girls; especially if she had a full workload the next day.

Sometimes Henri would get the receptionist to cancel his appointments for a couple of days. Where he went, she did not know. She really did not care. She was just thankful to have the girls and the office to herself.

He was a wreck gone wild.

Chapter 17

Meanwhile back at the Estate – Petra, Naomi, Maria and the 2 Peters are enthusiastically enjoying each others company. Oh yes, and by now Petra is well acquainted with Maria. She is often with them on excursions and for Wednesday Evenings.

Petra is charmed by Grandad's presence at Naomi's house. "He is Who He Is' when they are together. He is funny and fun to be with. A Wise and Understanding man. He could not hurt a flea.

That is obvious at the Estate House.

Yes, Petra continued to have the evening meal there, as Mara expected her to. So, she did whenever her and Peter were not planning something together. Grandad was very controlled in Mara's presence. She guessed he had learned long ago that though she calls him 'My Peter' it really did not mean much as far as love and affection went from her end. It was word only, perhaps to keep herself in the luxury she experienced as a Bokamosa.

Petra wondered if Mara's inner self were crying for exposure so she could BE integrous? Maybe she had too many hidden secrets. Maybe she lived in fear of being found out? Maybe even now, she is fearful of anyone finding out her relationship with Dr. Gardener in 'my Peter's' Estate House?

Petra had learned that the only child Grandad had fathered was Mayana Lucy, the youngest. She was born a year after his father David Bokamosa had died. His Little Lucy, a precious daughter that died by the time she was eleven.

At Naomi's they all played local games and shared a LOT OF HISTORY. Petra finds out too, that Peter and Mara's Marriage was 'an arranged marriage'. Arranged by Peter's father. No one was telling, but she got the impression that maybe David was Great Grandfather Bokamosa son. And Henri as well. Of course, they looked like Family.

The clue?

Grandad slipped in once that Petra may have arrived 3 weeks too early – full term, but David arrived 3 months too early – full term.

****

They all knew that Mara was up to something. But had not clued into the fact that she was intent on forcing Petra back to Canada.

"Where she belonged".

Petra had not heard much from her folks since she left for South Africa. They were busy with their lives as usual. It did not surprise her that her texts were seldom answered. But then, mostly she had just sent a photo of where they had been, an emoticon or two of love.

She saw that her mother had read or at least opened hers and occasionally sent a heart or two. Henri had not. Petra also knew that Mother was extremely taxed to the max with Patient Load, taking over Henri's appointments when he decided he could not show up for work along with his moody personality, and worries about Sara on the street.

Far away Petra knew she was probably the least of her mother's worries. She was glad for whatever it was that kept her in tune with her own InnerNet, so she was not a burden on anyone.

Well, accept Mara it seemed.

Petra wanted 'No Memories that <u>tainted her future</u>'. What Power gave her those feelings, she did not know, BUT she was very thankful for it.

(But then she had ONE that haunted her when she least expected it to.) Like a ghost in the night even here at Naomi's she would wake in a panic. She hoped it would leave her soon.

Petra was looking forward to the Winter/Summer Holidays in South Africa. Peter and Maria had planned to fly with her to the area where her Mother's family were from.

Mother never spoke of them. And when Petra had inquired, Mother would simply say "They mean nothing to me, Petra. It is just as well to leave dead lions buried." Obviously, Mother had some hidden pieces of history she was unwilling to face.

Even if this holiday was nothing more than a holiday, Petra was looking forward to travel with at least two people that seemed to appreciate who she was for who she was without preconceptions and judgements. It would be wonderful to have some space between Mara and herself. Maybe she could clue into Mara's resentment toward her and be more capable of tolerating her criticisms.

She wondered, "WOW! how did Grandad do it?"

Ah yes, he took comfort in Bob and Naomi over the years.

Sounds like Bob was a soulmate to Grandad until he died. Not only Naomi, Maria and Peter were by his side as he slipped into eternity after a stroke, three years before she came back to Johannesburg, but Grandad was there too.

Petra would have loved to have met him in older years. She remembered him as the Big Black Man in the Gardens. He was always kind to her and explained the background why to each Rose – why it had a certain name and number, and where it came from in the world. It all fascinated her, but for the life of her now she could not remember which was what. Then again, she was less than nine years old when he gave her the info.

It sounds like he just got sweeter as he got older. Maybe something like Grandad. Maybe because he loved Creation as the Creator created it – without man's tampering ways.

Maybe because of the way Naomi's LOVE was Capital, she loved them both the same. Of course, there would have been intimacy with Bob that there was not with Grandad, but that was beside the point.

Naomi LOVED!

Maybe that is why Grandad and Naomi had such a relaxing relationship. They were also closer to the same age than he and Mara were. He was twenty-six and Mara just fourteen the day of their wedding. Great Grandfather David's arranging. (Petra wondered if it was to cover his own lust?)

Grandad Peter joked "my folk must have thought they would never have grandchildren if they did not arrange it their way.
After all, I loved the prospect of what those crystal looking rocks could become more than people. People manipulated you into their ways of thinking. Whereas I oversaw manipulating the stones into something of Beauty."

Between Grandad and Naomi, there was something of Beauty.
No competition. No need to be better (or worst) than. Nothing hidden, simply TRANSPARENT.

Oh yes! Living from their own Integrity. Not afraid to BE who they were Created to BE! Created in the Likeness and Image of LOVE.

All things Petra wanted to remember when, if ever, she moved back to Canada – moved away from these wonderful influencers.

(well, except, for Mara. Then again, the contrast so great, it was a lesson all its own.) The new Gardener was 'A Live In'.

Mara had the end of the hall rooms converted to a Suite. It was obvious Peter was not going to remove Bob and Naomi from the Gate House for someone younger to garden. She was not going to hire one of those 'come and go' companies that work in many gardens to contaminate *Her Gardens*. Mara took pride in the appearance of The Estate.

There was an outside entry besides the door to the hall through the house. Henri's room had been left as part of the main house, and that is where Petra was lodged.

Mara knew him from the Horticulture Club she belonged to for years. He was not a young man, but apparently an accomplished Horticulturalist. He had emigrated from India with his parents when he was a teen. *So, he said.*

This was like his Retirement job. A place to live that he did not have to pay rent for and that came with *perks*.

Mara seemed quite happy with the arrangement.

Grandad saw no need to comment one way or the other. If Mara was happy, he had no complaints. However, 'my Peter' saw the crack between the Mask and the Face.

Now get this **Dr. David Gardener** PhD by name!

He was probably twenty, twenty-five years younger than Grandad, and Mara could not say enough about his wonderful abilities 'in the Gardens'.

Chapter 18

It was the end of November. Things had cooled off, and it rained most of the time. Marabella saw that Henri had extra D3 and a few other things at this time of year. In her mind he also suffered from SAD (Seasonal Adaptive Disorder).

They had the gas fireplace going, and for once in a lifetime, they had a quiet Friday evening to enjoy a good read. Deep into the Stories they chose to read, the phone rang. Neither answered. The 3rd time it started ringing again, they decided it must be an emergency. Someone certainly wanted to get their attention. Henri rose and pressed the Speaker Button so that they both would hear.

It was the Hospital in a nearby town. They had a Sara Bokamosa in Emergency and needed signatures as her ID signified Henri as NOK -next of Kin. If he could give the doctors a verbal Okay, they would proceed with what must be done immediately, and Henri could sign when they got there. Henri Okayed Proceedings. After all, Sara was his favorite feminine.

Quickly, they donned appropriate clothing and headed out in the rain. Henri was driving. Why was she in another town? Yes, they had lost track of her and had hoped that she was OK.

Henri placed his phone in the dash holder in case of another call. Marabella noticed it flashing. Some TEXTs from South Africa. So, as Henri drove, she began to read "Just to update you, I thought you should know that I am sure your daughter here is 'with child'. She has been spending a lot of time with The Professor Peter." Marabella heard Henri gasp.

"Never heard of this fellow. You seem to know something I do not sir?" quizzed Marabella.

"We have plenty to deal with right now with Sara in Emergency" Henri said. "We'll deal with Petra when we get through this. It cannot be that important. My mother likes gossip." You can say that again! Marabella knew her too well. Another reason for their moving away from Africa. So, she closed the phone and concentrated on the darkness through the rain splashed windshield.

20 minutes later, they arrived at the Hospital, entering through the night entry. It was 11:34 p.m., exactly a half hour after receiving the call, noted Henri.

They were ushered to a waiting area and Henri was given a Clipboard to sign. Sara was in the process of having her stomach pumped. It seemed she had taken an overdose of some heart medication. Whatever for? Many questions.

The minutes ticked into hours. Finally, the surgeon came in to explain the situation and the procedures. The Fetus was struggling for life and the heart rate was sporadic, so they had to do a C-Section to see if they could save the baby as it was full term. It had suffered too much stress.

A baby? This was a shock to Marabella and yet Henri seemed to know.

They had pumped Sara's stomach. Sara had held the baby as tiny as it was."

Two hours later, they were taken to the Palliative Care Unit. They questioned this but were told it was the best they could do in an emergency of this magnitude.

Sara was sleeping but hooked up to IVs and monitors. They both watched the monitors for several seconds. This does not look good!

Marabella moved to the bedside and took Sara's free hand. Henry put his hand on her knee. And then without warning, Sara awakened. She was coherent for a few minutes.

"Please don't let me die? I only wanted to take one but so many fell out. My back hurt so bad! Please Daddy tell me you won't let me die?" The effort was almost too much for Sara, and she passed out into fitful sleep.

Over the next 3 days, this was the pattern. Deep sleep with muttered words and attempt to scream; then a few moments of coherence before falling back into sleep or delirium.

Now that she was dying, it was obvious that Sara changed her mind and desperately wanted LIFE.

Marabella sat through it. Henri came and went. They were both hearts broken.

At one point, in her delirium, Sara became very demanding "where is my baby?"

"Bring me my baby?"

"Why did you kill my baby?"

"I know you did. Where is she?"

Later, when Sara was coherent, she said quietly "will I see my Baby in Heaven?" By this time, she was resigned to the fact that she was dying.

Then even more quietly *"It was Daddy's Baby you know.* I really miss her. She was so soft and so tiny. Please God let me hold her in Heaven."

Marabella had a pile of questions she dares not ask. Especially at such a fragile time. She would wait until the time was right.

Soon Sara slept again. Her breath getting softer and softer until it was no more. Henri noticed the clock 11:34 p.m. – Sunday evening. They quietly sat with Sara for several minutes before either moved.

Obviously, the monitor notified the Nursing Station, as the door flew open.

Robotically, Henri and Marabella did the final details the Hospital required to release Sara and the baby's body.

Drove their weary bodies and mind home in silence. Marabella drove as Henri was shaking too much for her to trust his driving skills. He did that every once in awhile.

Over the next few days in Robotic Action, they made the cremation plans for both bodies. Sara asked that their ashes be fertilizer for a certain Oak Tree in the park nearby.

Dr. Price, new in the City had filled in at the Clinic for them while they got their life back again. It is not easy to lose a child at any age.

It is less easy when you know you had a part in the death. That is how Henri acknowledged it all. He required recovery time.

The Insurance Company deposited the Life Insurance sum within three days. (They had kept Insurance Policies on their girls, as well as themselves, ever since they moved to Canada.)

With that, the 'Sara File' was closed and placed in Archives.

Chapter 19

Jamie - This morning, where do we start with LOVE? We are studying the Human Needs. Connection – LOVE – Appreciation

I feel like I have had so much of this, that I really do feel for the folks, including family who have not felt this Deep Abiding LOVE I feel from within. I am thankful that at an incredibly young age I felt the Connection to an InnerNet that has always been and always will be. A circle of LOVE that Creates the Peace this world is looking for in someone or something else outside of themselves.

Where shall I start?

Maybe the Bokamosa Diamond Mine when Grandad Peter would keep me on days both my parents were busy. Yes, my toys were rocks – bright shiny rocks. He had a special box for Sara and me to play with. I know now that they were chunks of Diamond rock big enough that we could not swallow. He would be busy working at his desk or counter or talking on the phone.

Sometimes men would bring a particularly small rock to him and ask him questions.

I remember he would respond with something like "That looks like a 24 carrot" or something like that. I would have to rise from the floor and see what the thing was that he called 24 carrot? My little mind would wonder how grandad could make 24 carrots out of a rock.

When we moved to Canada, I felt like I lost a LOVE Source. Soon I found parks and flowers and sometimes trips to the mountains as my comfort. My parents were extremely busy.

Since we were school age it did not matter so much. BUT I missed Grandad Peter. I had no one to talk about the bully at school or the teacher not understanding my accent. I did not know I had an accent, but these strangers in my new land certainly did.

The Library became my constant companion. Books my delight. The characters therein my Friends. Then one day it happened. In the Library my first year in the High School, a boy came and sat across the table from me. Goodness, there were a raft of other tables empty that he could have stopped at.

Well, that is when I began to understand the LOVE that two people could have for each other. To say the least, Petri made me feel connected to another human being. Yes, I would never forget my connection to the InnerNet. Maybe that connection made Petri and mine more significant. I could LOVE and feel LOVE without it having to come from a person in flesh and blood. But a person in body added a special element to LOVE.

I glanced up and saw that he had chosen the same book I was studying "A Course in Miracles". He too was looking at me with a big smile to match my own. I would say it was LOVE at first sight. A LOVE I thought would last forever. It did for at least three years until after graduation when we both left on a Monday morning for destinations far apart.

Why we never thought to get contact information, I have never figured out. I am wondering if he might have the same feelings. I sometimes wonder if I will ever meet him again.

And then I arrive in South Africa to find at least four Loves of my life. How blessed I am!

Arriving back in Canada with a couple of LOVEs by my side, I was fearful that once they left, I would be totally alone as far as humans go. I was comforted when I corrected my perspective and remembered I would never be far from my Creator's Eternal LOVE.

Chapter 20

Next – The Petra File

The Petra Issue had been placed on the back burner for a few weeks. Now there was a whole wack of emails and texts from Mara. Certainly, she was determined to get Petra out of South Africa or at least off the Estate.

Petra was all but 21. She was a Woman. By now, it was right to give her Freedom to Claim responsibility. However, when one has compromised their 'Who I Am' to keep Peace in the Family, it does not appear to be that easy. Especially when someone else is paying the shots. Often, we feel trapped in *the Chain Breaking Process*.

Though Mara wanted all Ties Broken to Petra, she did not recognize the fact that Not Petra but she herself was tightening the Chain lest her own secrets be revealed.

Mara was not a happy camper with Peter paying so much attention to Petra. Petra had even taken to sleeping at Naomi's place. Or was she sleeping at Peter's? She had a ton of evidence that Petra was not a good girl; and here 'my Peter' had paid to bring her to the Estate House. For how long, Mara wondered?

Petra just could not endure Mara's rants about her filthy behavior with that Peter fellow. Of course, she knew Mara interpreted it as sleeping with Peter. If she only knew and could accept the TRUTH!

Mara said that Peter Senior was upset enough that he would not pay for Petra's flight home. (though both Henri and Marabella knew clearly that Peter NEVER got upset).

Methodically as everything was these days in overwhelm, Marabella went about getting Travel arrangements together for Petra to come home when her current curriculum was completed. Mailed the Tickets to Petra, but not before Henri included a letter. Marabella never bothered to read it. She had no more energy to protect anyone else from the other.

Marabella went back to work. With the assistance of Dr. Price, she could bring closure to the sad Sara and granddaughter chapter of her life.

Henri claimed he needed time, so she left all the other arrangements to him since he was not going back to work for a long time yet. Sometimes she wished she could bring Closure to the Henri File as well. But she felt sorry for him.

Henri called "3 Strong Guys" to haul Petra's furniture and belongings out to the cabin. They might as well eliminate both girls' rooms at the same time and proceed with plans of their own. They could each have a 'Home Office' or hobby room where the girl's rooms had been.

His generosity arranged with the accountant to deposit $5000 a month living allowance into an account for Petra. They could do so out of Sara's Insurance Money.

He even went so far as to get the Lawyer to draw up documents that allowed Petra to change her name to whatever it was, she wished. After all, he found out years ago when he did the DNA Science Experiment that she was not his DNA.

Once they were sure that Petra would stay in Canada, and not bring Peter or Maria here, they would sign the cabin property over to her. But first they must be sure of her good intentions.

He assumed Mara's assumptions were correct, and they could hardly believe their submissive daughter Petra had so defiled her up bringing.

Overwhelm can create a lot of unfortunate beliefs within us.

He arranged for the Uber Driver to meet the Airlines and deliver Petra the 5 hours out to the cabin. Neither had thought about the Airport less than 20 minutes from the Cabin.

He arranged with Willow Wisdom to attend to Petra's needs.

They would pay her to do so.

ALL ARRANGEMENTS MADE

– THE FILE CLOSED

Except that it could not be Archived like Sara's.

Petra was still very much alive.

Chapter 21

Jamie – I am back for another chapter of learning. Peter is busy with his studies and I am free for a while longer to study for myself or is it to assist my Clients and Reading Tribe?

Creativity – Growth

How does Growth Happen?

Growth happens through Experience. Creativity happens through the way we interpret the Experiences. Is it Curiosity Fueling our Ship? Curiosity and Observation are excellent Fuel.

Will Power can accomplish a lot, but it is Force and force loses momentum over time.

Look how children create and grow physically, mentally, and emotionally. They are mostly driven by Curiosity. By observation, they learn the Burner is HOT, won't touch it next time.

Another observation – Birds fly but I do not. Squirrels climb fast but I am too Big to climb in those small branches and so on.

What are the Talents you have that others may not? What do you do well that you could share with the world?

What is your Hair Out of Place – the thing you could do all day and get lost in, and yet are questioned about by others?

I received a Fortune Cookie which read: "You have the ability to seek out Higher Truth and Relate it in Simplicity."

Yes, I had recognized that a few years before. So, what do I do now? Coach by following that very message. I listen carefully and interpret what a person is saying in a way that they understand their own message even better.

It is *my Hair Out of Place.* The thing I do best, but is least understood by others...

I am also a Perpetual Learner – I devour deep things and then use the methodology in its simplest form to inform my Clients.

This is my area of Growth and Creativity. Of course, I am also Artistically Creative as in Painting, Writing and Designing. You have your own specialty.

Perhaps animals and animal wellness are your interest. Maybe Science, Fashion and Fabric, Social Worker – you will know what you can do everyday all day long and lose yourself in it.

And yes, maybe get paid for something you would love to do with out pay.

www.strengthsfinder.com is a good place to start.

I found my 5 Top Strengths; and now understand why it appears that I am always looking for another course to indulge in. My number one strength is LEARNER.

Chapter 22

The whole picture changed in South Africa 14 days into December.

Peter was waiting for a certain Bank Note to mature the end of November before he Booked their flights to Cape Town. He would have it all settled before the end of November.

It was a Gift of Appreciation for Maria, Naomi, and Petra. Three Amazing Women he was lucky enough to have nurture him in ways he had no words to describe. He would include a Surprise Event just for Petra. Each one in their own unique way brought Life and Light to his Living.

Maria was only Fifteen years his senior. Grandma was forty-five when he was born. Maria being her only child. And now Petra who was less than ten years younger. All could climb a Mountain together he was sure. They were all continually active physically.

When Peter was school age, Maria had become a Fitness Coach – 25 years later, she was still going strong. Naomi continued to help in the Gardening at the Estate, though mostly just the veggie gardens closest to her house.

Even Grandad could be found in the cool of evening picking what was required for a delicious meal if that were where he found Naomi.

Grandad had been so good to Peter, that Peter thought strongly about including him in this excursion to Petra's relatives on the other side, and literally distance wise too.

However, when Senior Peter was consulted, he understood the magnitude of the invitation, but declined saying "I don't count much anymore in the Estate House over there, but Mara would be some upset if I ignored Christmas with her."

"Afterall, it is the only time of year I allow her to manipulate me into that Church building."
He then added "show off *'my Peter'*! Ya know". Then with a chuckle "I know I ain't he anymore. Might not even matter to her this year, but I sense in my bones *she not very happy with none of us* right now. And besides that, I have a few Secrets up my sleeve to deliver before year end."

And it was left at that.

Friday, December 14, the Sun was shining, but not too hot. Summer was entering and Petra was thankful she was not in the Rainy Season on the West Coast of the north this year.

What a Gorgeous Day in Paradise!

In a week, the Holiday would begin. Final exams would keep both her and Peter occupied. Time would pass very quickly.
Peter had booked an Evening Flight for December 21. That way, they would not be wasting precious tour time. They would be gone exactly 2 weeks, arriving back after the New Year.

They would miss Mara's New Years bash, but none seemed to care deeply as they would have their own celebration on the other side of the continent. And little could they even guess the Magnitude of that Celebration!

Mara loved entertaining on a Grand Scale. Each year she held a huge Party with Fireworks on New Years Eve – a kind of thank you to all her friends and relatives.

Oh yes, she included the folks that worked on the Estate as well.

'Good for All Races and Wages to mix, you know!'

Maybe it was her way of remembering her days of poverty and abuse without remembering.

And then the Bomb was DROPPED! She had mail for Petra.

It came in a Brown Envelop like the one from Grandad's Desk drawer addressed to Jamie. But this was addressed to Petra Karabo. Not even to Petra Karabo-Bokamosa.

There was no return address either. Strange!

It included Sara's Funeral card.

It held Petra's Flight Tickets back to Victoria for the evening of December 21.

It was her car keys – apparently already at the Cabin.

It was a VISA Gift Card in case she required meals along the way.

How insane!

The letter accompanying this was written on Henri's office stationery. *Very 'official'*.

Three pages of 'Sorry and Apology'. Oh my! Marabella's name was not attached to any of this accept as a parent of Sara.

Here is the gist of it all.

To All Whom this may concern:

We are extremely sorry that Petra played the fool with Peter. Something we had never dreamed of when she left for South Africa.

Mom, we got your text on our way to the hospital the very day that Sara died. We are heart broken and see no solution except for Petra to return home ASAP.

It is something to grieve for someone now gone and in eternity. It is something even more devastating to find that a child you had great hopes for as a Doctor, had damaged her future in such a way, especially when we supplied the necessary protection for it not to happen.

We are so sorry that Petra has insulted in so many ways, Mom. Since she has always been a submissive child, this is very out of character and surprising to us both. But then I must remember that she is no longer a CHILD."

We feel so sorry for the dreadful activity of our daughter, and sorry that you felt so much overwhelm Dad that you could not pay Petra's way home when you had paid to get her to South Africa in the first place.

We do not want to see Maria and Peter following Petra back, therefore we are sending the tickets. Fortunately, Sara's Life Insurance came through, to do this. The Tickets are not to be altered and must be used.

We do not wish for any tampering with these arrangements in any way. We have arranged for transportation since she will be arriving when we are at Whistler skiing.

Peter and Petra had best delete their Engagement. We will deal with the pregnancy when Petra returns as to what is best.

105

Sincerely,

Dr. Henri Bokamosa

And that was it!

Grandmother Mara seemed delighted.

Grandad could hardly believe his senses as Petra read the letter aloud to them both in tears.

Petra was dumb struck. She had told no one of her suspicions from within. Who would believe her? Especially not Mara.

She stuffed the items back into the envelop and quickly exited Mara's dining room for Naomi's, where she again read the letter to all three since they were eating together. Maybe they could help her make sense of this devastation.

Maria seemed to know that this is how Henri and Mara dealt with a lot of things.

– reek havoc at the least expected moment.

Peter was petrified. What could he say? He felt like he was an accomplice in The Crime, but had no idea of how?

Or even what the crime was?

Naomi's wisdom simply wrapped them all in a Blanket of LOVE. She had been through all this more than once since Mara entered the Bokamosa Estate through the Very Proud David Bokamosa; an Event that had changed her own destiny as well.

She still felt for Mayana, his lovely wife whom he seldom appreciated. Peter senior was her only child that survived birthing. Peter was always close to his mother. He had her quiet and loving nature.

The evening of December 21 Grandad would take them all to the airport. Fortunately for Petra, they would be on the same flight to Cape Town. Then Petra would catch her connecting flight across the sea as she understood it.

All would say their Goodbyes with heavy hearts. And most of all, they felt for Grandad going back to bear the burden of his household by himself until they returned.

Sadness filled her heart. Grandad was getting old. Would she ever have opportunity to see him again? Their Hearts had united in the few months they had together.

Life happens according to what we choose from deep within our subconscious, but the HOW comes in ways we do not expect. She knew that somehow this would all work toward her own Integrity Growth. In unexpected ways possibly.

Look at the growth in Grandad – he was not much older than her when his world was turned upside down in a *marriage arranged* instead of with his beloved Naomi.

Grandad is nobody's fool. He left with his backpack without even helping Mara with the clean up. He let Saturday and Sunday guide him. He went quietly away to his own Sanctuary in Nature. No, it was not in the Estate Gardens.

He planned and played the fairest game possible to be a Win/Win/Win for everyone involved. He did not use his head like most men do. A Heart-InnerNet Connection would open The Way.

At this time, more than any in his life, he required the Guidance of the Holy Spirit (Heart-InnerNet as his Jamie called it) to direct and give him the answers as to how to correct the misjudgements in this situation.

There were Miracles unimaginable ahead.

He Lived from His Integrity InnerNet.

The above could have been The End!

But not if Peter Bokamosa Sr. had anything to do with this outcome. He could not let those he LOVED to be 'railroaded' into sadness of heart. He would call on all the helps he could to create a better outcome from his LOVE.

Too often he had seen this pattern of later regret. He would not let it happen to his Beloved Granddaughter now. Time was ticking and he had lots to do.

So, he desperately required the time alone. Only Naomi knew where he had gone Friday evening after supper.

Chapter 23

Naomi and Peter Senior had less than a week to draw a more acceptable conclusion to this scam and encourage the younger generations with the WISDOM that is higher than Church.

They came up with a plan. If it all aligned, with the Integrity of The InnerNet, The Grace of The Creator; Peter jrs. plan could be fulfilled.

No, it would not meet approval from *Dr. Henri Bokamosa, Mara Bokamosa, and the Horticulture Professor.* They both doubted that Marabella was consulted much about the arrangements though she seldom questioned Henri's decisions.

Peter might be considered old, but he knew a thing or two about Business, Airports and all that insignificant stuff. He knew his way around people and situations in a LOVE driven positive way. He called on all he could at the time.

The Assignment in Alignment he gave Naomi was to present Petra with yet another Brown Envelop as soon as they entered the Airport.

The second Assignment in Alignment was to guide Petra into Being a Fully Responsible Woman of Wisdom to choose for herself the future she so desired.

How?

Well, Grandad did not sit idle once he was back early Monday morning. He had less than a week to do His Own Assignment in Alignment.

Petra, in her unbelief had left the envelop on Naomi's table. Grandad had all he required. First, he called the airlines and asked to change Petra's Flight out of Cape Town for January 6.

Then he brought it to their attention that his granddaughter was booked twice for the same flight, by different people from Johannesburg to Cape Town. He had Peter's ticket for her transferred to another name and date. He was sure Peter jr. would agree.

As it was, the Airline had 2 seats left on the Atlantic portion of the flight January 6 besides having bumped Petra forward. He booked both seats and paid the rest for the tickets. He could always cancel later.

Petra would see the others leave Cape Town and have a couple of days to herself to search her own Heart-InnerNet. Peter senior wanted to make sure the choice to return to Canada was her own and not forced upon her. If she wished to fly back to Johannesburg, he would support her decision and make it possible.

There would be no extra charge, because the flight Petra would have been on out of Cape Town, was being cancelled. Petra would use the Ticket Henri sent to get to Cape Town. Grandad would use Peter's ticket after the new year.

He and Naomi rejoiced together.

Mara need not know of any of this. It made it even easier because for some reason, the end of November, Petra had asked Naomi and Grandad permission to move over to Naomi's place.

Grandad wondered Why? He would not ask. If he needed to know, it would filter back to him gently through Naomi.

Second, Grandad took to looking at the Uber Card. Five hours of road travel after a long flight seemed a might too much for a young woman to him. He questioned whether a young woman would be safe traveling with a complete stranger in winter rains. He had so many questions about the hideous Henri plan.

He believed there must be airports closer. He went online and did some exploration of his own. What about the Airport just outside of Tofino?

He looked at the time, and the time in Victoria. It was early enough he could make the Call. Though Grandad had to put it on Speaker so Naomi could help him understand the accent on the other end, they managed to make the necessary arrangements for the driver to pick Petra up a few days later. They would get back to him with a location closer to the time.

It did seem the driver was a bit agitated at the change since it would be in a different year. They also asked the driver if he had the phone number for the Lady who would be at 'the cabin' to be with Petra when she arrived? He did and courteously gave it to them.

Before Peter finished, he had a hunch – he asked, "Are there airport connections from Victoria to the Tofino Airport?" Peter thanked the Driver and said he would get back to him with further arrangement once they knew all was aligned.

They hung up the phone, and Peter smiled to Naomi "It's our Lucky Day Sister!"

Grandad also added "Naomi if you find that Petra is pregnant and it is Peter the father, then by all means make sure you assure her she is welcome back. Please make sure she understands that she is Twenty-one and has full legal right to make all her own decisions."

He remembered too well the trap he had been taken in years ago; though he no longer let it define him or interfere with his happiness in the moment. Forgiveness is rewarding.

He stared out the window for a long time. He saw the gardener riding the mower in a distance. He did not have a good feeling about this fellow. But then who was he to have any say anymore.

Mara saw him as 'in the way' so he simply did his own business and spent a lot of time here at Naomi's, even if it was simply reading a book, he never used to have time for.

He brought himself back to the present.

"Naomi, you will have a lot to research on the plane and at Cape Town. I know your gentle ways can bring the best out of this Precious Young Woman. I don't believe for a moment that Petra and Peter have defiled anyone, not even themselves."

I am starting to wonder if that bedroom is Possessed though? That is where my own father took Mara more than once. That's where Henri took your Maria."

"And now? You know Naomi, just between you and I, Petra requesting your empty bedroom makes me very suspicious, that *if she is 'with child'* it is that Gardner."

"I have my doubts he is who he says he is. I started a Private Investigation several months ago. I wondered what his birth certificate says for name and age?"

"Oh yah! He can keep Mara happy where I can not, being pleasured is her aim I recon."

Grandad stood up and stretched. He needed a walk in the Garden himself. His anger was getting a grip that might slug the guy. He suggested that Naomi accompany him to the mine for a walk around.

He knew he still had Willow to communicate with, but that would wait until later, or even tomorrow. It was as if he were afraid that even Naomi's house might be bugged or have secret cameras.

Ah! Cameras?

Yes, they would bring home the last of his stuff from the locked securities room. Even more reason to take Naomi with him.

He needed space between himself and the Estate. He needed to come up with a way of identification. Petra had told no one she was pregnant. She did not have to. The nausea was probably enough. Naomi had noticed it about a week after she moved over.

Now, this might sound strange, but Grandad had the surveillance cameras at the Estate aligned with his computer in the Securities Closet at work. Mostly, that in the days of their instillation, both he and Mara were often working at the mine.

If anything were going on at the estate, that Bob and Naomi missed, could be observed, and addressed immediately.

Of late they had been almost ignored. He did not want to see what was going on when he was not there. But just now, he was curious to see if the camera just outside Petra's window was on and if it could detect anything.

If her curtains were open, highly likely they would have evidence. Because the windows faced gardens and not likely that anyone would be looking, few of the curtains at the house were ever drawn.

Peter had locked the large closet where the computer with the cameras on was. The one room he had not yet released to the new owners. He was not sure why he had not hauled it all to the Gate House a couple weeks earlier when he had Peter's strong arms to help?

Providence maybe had created the circumstance for this very reason. Mara had her curtains drawn a lot since Dr Gardener arrived on premise, which was not surprising.

However, Peter sr. was most interested in three specific cameras. The end of the hall, which had 3 lenses – one focused on the room Petra slept in, the others focused on each end of the hall. The camera one outside Petra's window; and the one above the Suite entrance from outside could give him clues.

Part way there, he said "You know Naomi this little jaunt is more than I thought at the outset. We are going to investigate the surveillance system at the house. Might give us some clue as to the reason Petra left that bedroom. She likely had good reason – more than just ghosts of the past."

"It might give us a head start to find out her underlying sadness even though she presents a very controlled front." They both agreed that Petra was wearing a Mask the past month. What had happened to persuade her to move over to Naomi's? They both believed it was more than Mara getting on her nerves.

Petra seemed happy enough when she was with the rest of them in an evening. But every once in awhile, it was like a Mask – a haunted look swept over Petra and a shake or shiver of her body made them uncomfortable – not to be around her, but to know something had changed her countenance?

She would take a deep breath and resume her sweet smile.

Just in case anything should be lost in the disconnecting of the devices, they sat down and viewed the cameras for the end of November – when Maria, Peter, and Petra had returned from the Safari. That was about when Petra asked to be moved.

There it was! It did not take long. Naomi gasped "Peter that is the very night the kids returned from the Safari. I bet she was exhausted."
That being said, and Peter seeing that hideous lunatic face of the gardener as he went out the door – imagine making a face at a security camera! Indeed, the man was a 'mad man'. Peter made a memory stick of the whole month of November and to date before they disconnected and loaded the equipment into the truck.

Between the two of them, they managed to pack up the tiny room and its computers and cameras. They would establish them in Grandad's New Office at the Gate House.

When they got back to Naomi's, Grandad called Willow Wisdom. He could not wait another day. He told her the situation.

Willow told him of the Airport just minutes away from the cabin – in fact, you must drive around the end of the airport to get to the Cabin from any direction other than by water.

He also informed her that if Petra chose to go along with the arrangements, she would likely arrive on January 7 or 8 instead. He asked Willow to keep the change to herself. He did not wish for Petra's parents to be involved in the new arrangement.

Willow seemed to understand. There was no hesitation in the flow of their conversation. It was almost like he was talking to Naomi, but with a Canadian Accent.

FINISHED!

This is not the End.

It is only the Beginning.

Eternal LOVE is like that!

Book Two picks up as to Who Flew Where – BIG question we all are Curious?

Is Petra 'with child', if so, whose?

The Rest of The Story.

Join us in

Book II

"Trans Parent Alignment"

Owning Alignment with Our **Integrity InnerNet**!

Beyond education, parent, political and socially trained beliefs.

Before the great **ADULT**eration.

Back to the LOVE that created the child!

We left Four people at the Airport in Johannesburg, South Africa. Peter Senior had dropped them off and went home to endure Mara and Dr. Gardener for the Christmas Holidays – without the Support of those he counted Dear.

We are all wondering 'Who went where?'

Was Petra pregnant?

What about Jamie, Peetteri, Jack and the rest of the gang?

Do Petra and Petri's lives ever cross again?

What about the relationship with Mara, Dr. Gardener and Peter Senior?

Or even Peter Junior and Petra's relationship?

This book answers all the above.

Now please join me again Dear Reader.

Chapter 1

Compelling Future Not Driven by Will Power

Driven by Enthusiastic Curiosity

My Compelling Future began for me out of Tragic Circumstances. Who would have thought that being raped – being with child as a result – being totally misunderstood and shipped away to an isolated place by family could create a Compelling Future?

Well, a lot of my Clients come to me from these or similar circumstances as well. Perhaps that is why I am sought out as a Coach. Because I have experience in seeing the other side of what they are experiencing I have credibility in assisting them in their Journey to the Other Side – to Their Own Compelling Future.

Two things that often accompany sexual trauma are either or together Overweight to hide our 'Attractiveness' and/or Depression. For myself, it was depression. I still ride that rollercoaster as hormonal changes go through the month.

However, I have come to understand the cycle and ride it through by Being Aware of the thought patterns and dietary requirements to minimize the down. There is a week each month that I know I would not choose wisely. Thus, I avoid any major decisions at that time.

Also, I have a Biorhythm App to follow my Life Cycles on. It is important when planning for Live Events. By referencing the biorhythms, I recognize what days I will be the Best Teacher.

Willow and I coordinate our UP Rhythms as much as is possible for 2 people to do. At our best, and above the days that may include a tint of depression, we Flow Best and are more likely to focus on our accolades rather than the critic in the class.

Yes, there was a time that I was driven by Will Power. My good behavior and Fit-in ability as a child. My study habits in school because I could not keep up with a language and teaching methods I was not used to, took a lot of will power to endure. And that is exactly what will power does – takes endurance.

But then all things changed after Peter was conceived, and I was given Pictures to Paint and Books to Write. My Talents to perfect and share. The humility to simply hold the brush or allow my fingers to type the words that sometimes I do not understand myself.

All of which is Compelling.

Is Curiosity Driven.

Sure, I have my opinions as to what the end should look like, just as I have my opinions about governing bodies and plandemic circumstances. BUT I know that when I let them go, I become calm and assured that All is Well in my World.

Fortunately, I learned the Ho'oponopono Teaching when I was a teen. It is a method of deliverance that I wish everyone to know. Forgiveness simply changes so much that could make our Future anything but Compelling.

Remember: Forgiveness is not for the other person as much as it is for oneself. The cleansing of our own Soul InnerNet.

My Future will be better than planned if I keep EGO and intellect calm, tamed to obey the orders of the InnerNet of Integrity and eternal LOVE.

What does your compelling future Look Like?

Smell Like?

Feel Like?

Sound Like? Etc.

Most of us know what we do not want from past experiences.

Get a bunch of magazines; go online and collect pictures of Compelling things.

Collect Words and Phrases that Inspire you. Collect them in a fancy box to begin with.

On the Box, print "My Compelling Future LOVES ME — This or something better is happening."

Eventually get a large Poster Board or magnetic Bulletin board to arrange the finds on. I like the Bulletin Board idea because I can add and take away when I have achieved the trait or object. Date when you placed it on your Board, and when you achieved the item. Place the item in the Box you emptied onto your Compelling Map. In the future, it is interesting to open the box and see how short the gestation period was for some of them.

Take photos of the Collage of your Compelling Future. Make the Photo the Background or Wallpaper the Computer Login, smartphone, print a few Business Card sizes to put in your wallet, etc.

Hang the large Collage where you will pass it often. Yes, glance at it as often as you can. However, the Flash of it as you pass it, will inspire you.

Once we know what we Desire, all our actions can incorporate movement into that Realm. If we do not know, we waste a lot of energy. With our Vision in place, we invest time and energy rather than wasting it.

One Client told us that simply the side vision of her Collage gives her giggles. Yes, she has achieved the Peace of Mind and the Occupation she hung on her board to name a couple.

The FUN is in the Frolic!

Chapter 2

He had come in so quietly.

Petra was in a very deep sleep.

Peter and Maria had taken her on a 3 Day Safari. When she got home, she had a shower and plopped into bed.

Sleep was instant.

But so were so many dreams. Dreams of the sights they had seen; animals they had encountered; and strangely visions of Henri and Maria in this very bed; and a glimpse of someone who looked like a young Mara with an old man she did not know; then a glimpse of Petri unlocking her car door – and more dreams.

Yes, she had learned Maria's story this past week. She could only feel sorry for Henri (and by now she was assured she had no blood connection). Maybe some of this info was being sorted in her Dream World.

As for Maria, it probably made her the strong, grounded, and intelligent Woman Petra had come to love and appreciate her wisdom. Interesting how the 'Bad Stuff' when not stuffed but brought to light becomes the LOVE that Lights the Soul. Like Grandad said:

'Another Facet Sparkling to the Beholder'.

But this? Was it real, or was she in a dream?

It was a hot summer night, and she needed no covers. She had simply left the towel wrapped loosely around her body.

Obviously, she had rolled out of it.

She sensed someone was on the bed, like she could feel the weight – an invisible being. She was lying on her stomach. She sensed that someone raised and was holding her hips up and entered.

She wondered if she Loved Petri and Peter enough to be having *'a wet dream'?*

She tried to move.

She tried to scream.

She only felt the friction, like something was where nothing had been before.

No Dream was this!

She felt the pressure for real!

She felt the pressure of his nails at the sides of her butt as he forced her back and forth along with his own thrust.

SILENT – No it was not consent.

Someone had invaded her privacy and she wanted to move, to scream to slug the guy.

Who was it?

She still could not get her head awake enough to move or take in what was real and what was not - to know.

And then he with drew with a toss of her body out of his way. Her body slumped back on the bed. She heard her door close.

She heard the hall door close and the lock click.

She KNEW.

She knew her virginity had been stolen.

STOLEN!

How could this be the conclusion of such a wonderful Weekend of FRIENDSHIP & FAMILY – Feeling a Deep sense of Family she was not familiar with before?

Petra was awake now.

Furious!

What a creep!

How dare he take advantage of her.

How dare he watch to take her off guard.

The wet! The sting! The slimy yuk!

More than anything, it stung her conscience.

It was this easy for a rape? (period)

Wide awake now, she got up to the bathroom and washed her private parts.

Still, she could not get them clean.

She heard the gardener's hideous laughter – distant, beyond walls. These walls were not insulated, or sound proofed.

She felt like vomiting, and she did.

She began to sob but tried to control the volume enough to keep from waking her grandparents. They likely would not hear, because they both had rooms at the other end of the house.

Finally, she just sat on the cool bathroom floor. Spent! In more ways than one.

How could she eventually tell that one who would place the Diamond on her finger that she was not pure?

Why was she *paralyzed and silent* when a scream would have been the answer? Scared him off?

Why did she have no muscle power, like an animal taken in the forest?

She wanted to tell somebody, EVERYBODY!

But who?

They would not believe her anyway.

Did she even believe herself?

How did she know it was him?

He could easily convince Mara of his own righteousness. That he had nothing to do with it and did not know what Petra was talking about. Besides Doors were locked.

OR were they?
And who had keys?

Mara trusted this man more than she trusted her granddaughter. What would her word mean? And she sure could not bear to tell Grandad. He was such a good man.

She began to berate herself. She was so weary when she got home. Had she even shut her door, let alone locked it?

Was he taking the hall route after visiting with grandparents or at least with Mara, and saw her lying there naked?

Had he taken it as an invitation that she wanted his attention?

She went and sat in the tub again trying to wash away the guilt, the anger, the frustration with being a Woman and having no RIGHTS.

She heard his hideous laughter again. She wished the walls were more solid. She put wet face cloths over her ears. Maybe she was just hearing it in her very confused head.

She pulled on heavy PJs even though it was still warm. Took a winter blanket from the closet in the bathroom to lay on and rolled up tight on the bathroom floor in another. She just could not make herself enter that room again this night. Thankful for an extra pillow in the closet as well.

Petra began her Ho'oponopono Prayer. Petra really wanted to shout it to drown out his laughter – maybe make him recognize his stupidity. Oh well! At least it would purify her own her Integrity InnerNet of LOVE.

I am sorry.
Please forgive me.
I love you.
Thank you.

She did not want to know how this could work in this situation. Her feelings as well as her flesh were too raw.

She wanted REVENGE.

But she asked anyway.

The Creator answered.

"Vengeance is mine. I will repay."

Her mind went to the Psalmist "do to mine enemies from your justice, O LORD."

Petra remembered the day she finally 'GOT' that verse.

God *Is LOVE*.

If God is LOVE, then His justice is LOVE.

I am sorry.
Please forgive me.
I love you.
Thank you.

She did not know what she was sorry for besides losing her virginity maybe – or had she lost it when she was little, when it happened in the playhouse at kindergarten?

She did not know who she was asking to Forgive – HER? Forgive her for what?

She did not know who she was saying 'I love you' too.

She did not know who she was Thanking.

However, it was enough to fall into a fitful sleep on the hard bathroom floor as the dreams continued – only now they were more like nightmares.

Petra was sure she screamed out loud in her sleep when the tiger pounced on her.

Chapter 3

With the house cleaned out of the children's stuff, Henri and Marabella decided to have it painted and redecorated by a professional. They had the money to do so out of Sara's Insurance.

Dr. Price had been filling in more and more for Henri. Henri seemed to be less and less capable of getting motivated to go to work. Marabella knew he was deeper than ever into a depression she could not, had never understood. She questioned the number of prescriptions he took.

The Whistler holiday seemed to relieve some of his grief; but as soon as they returned to work, it reappeared. They both agreed that Henri required time in a *Dry Out Center*. But where? He did not want to go anywhere in the greater Vancouver area or on the Island. He began to research.

Leipzig, SK kept coming into view. It was a Private Center, run by people who understood addiction. They were recovering themselves. It was an old Convent modified and brought up to date. It was a 7-week program with an extra week available if you wanted to integrate deeper.

It was not cheap, but then they had the money now. And one thing about it, it was in a remote location. His colleagues would not know his whereabouts. Appearance meant a lot to Henri even though he did not recognize that he was not making as good a one as he thought. People see through us.

The renos could wait. The next Group would be taken in January 21. It was full, but he would be put on a waiting list. If there was any cancellation, he would be called. He would not have much notification time.

The application was all online, and a Zoom Call arranged to face-view the applicant.

Dr. Price offered to buy Henri out. Marabella was all for it. Most of her patients were in the hospital, and that is where most of her time was spent. She did not require the expenses of a Downtown Clinic. Neither did Henri in her mind. But then there were a lot of things she did not think Henri needed that he thought *'they needed'*.

There was a twist though. Marabella had started her own Bank Account and separated her portion and expenses from Henri a couple of years prior. She sensed the day would come when all would be pulled from her. Already her daughters were.

Her earnings were higher than his, and that had started to irritate him. He was also disappearing for several days at a time. Where? She did not know. She had not been interested in finding out either.

He was a weird man!

Dr. Price was in favour of cutting two cheques as he understood the pressure Marabella was under. He understood too well. He had lived with a Narcissistic wife for too many years not to know. Sadly, she had cut her own life short.

They lived too close to the Falls along the North Saskatchewan River. The frozen falls was not a place you wore stiletto heels to walk on in the winter without a reason. Even sadder, was the fact that a group of teens found the lifeless body on the ice-covered rocks 50 feet below.

Price decided it was time to leave his practice in Alberta and find a warmer climate. His dreams haunted him, especially in winter, when the wind howled down the creek and out into the open river area. Its haunting sounds haunted his soul – what more could he have done to protect her from herself?

They had no children.

He was a free man and could go wherever his wondering feet took him. And so, it was Victoria. Fortunate to find a place to let go of the past and move on to something NEW.

While doing the legal work with the Lawyer to sell to Price they began to revise their Estate and Will as well. However, twist after twist after twist!

Would there never be a smooth road? Thought Marabella.

Of course, Sara died, and Dr. Price was even more in demand to cover for Henri. Marabella was more than grateful that Price's *Price* was Right and being processed before Henri really lost it!

Because the Cabin was clear of any indebtedness, and Petra would be soon returning, they went about having it signed over to her. But Henri wanted to wait for one more document he said, which would likely be available mid January for the 'correct landowner name'.

Out of Sara's Insurance, they set up a $5000 a month deposit to look after Petra's needs. With a kid on the way, how else was she going to look after things in an out of the way place. It would be cheaper than keeping them in Victoria. He was feeling very Generous.

Petra was a country girl and liked the sand, so why would she not be in favor of this plan? She could look after getting utilities into the place. Maybe she preferred not having running water in the house and having an outhouse.

Henri added "Oh by the way, I want to draw up papers for Petra to change her name to whatever she wants, since she is not a Bokamosa anyway; and since her conception was not of me at Petra."

This was in the Lawyer's Office. Marabella's mouth dropped. It would have been one thing for him to let her know his thoughts at home, but in front of a Lawyer! It was about enough for Divorce action on the spot after putting up with his garbage for more than twenty-one years now.

Silently Marabella would ride through this wave too. Eventually she would see her way free. How often in the hard times had her mind went to Ben – what would life have been with him instead of this lunatic man?

Yet he was an old man in her eyes at the time – he was 12 years her senior; yes, still handsome, and definitely a charming romantic. He finished his term teaching at the University as she finished her Residency. They both took totally different directions in the world from there. She had no desire to live in America – at least not yet at that time.

Marabella felt like she needed a break as well. Too many things piling up at one time.

Grief upon grief!

When would it end?

Sedona, Arizona sounded like just the place. No more expensive than Leipzig, but a place she could take a more relaxed and natural approach to look at her own 'stuffed emotions.' Miiamo here I come! https://www.miiamo.com/

(Deep down, she would like to have taken Petra with her. But she was pregnant.)

They had not heard from Willow, so they assumed that all was as planned.

They had not heard from Mara either. Usually, she would be informing them of Petra's farewell and assurance she was on the plane.

SILENCE!
– was Silence Good or Bad?

Chapter 4

Petra awakened to a distant alarm ringing. She was somewhat disorientated. Where was she? Quietly glancing around, she remembered her location.

Quickly and Quietly, she began again:

I am sorry.
Please forgive me.
I love you.
Thank you.

Then she added "Father forgive, they know not what they do."

If nothing else, it relaxed her frantic emotions. At least she would not Stone the guy when (and this was a when, not an if she saw him) Petra wondered if it would be easier if she did not know who it was?

STOP! STOP! STOP!

She silently screamed. She did not require a bad attitude to face another day.

And so,

I am sorry.

Please forgive me.
I love you.
Thank you.

"Father forgive, they know not what they do."

It would be her Mantra for the rest of her time here in this house and for as long as she required. Creator knows and that is all that matters right now. She must get through this day in the best possible way.

Mara wore on her nerves enough. Petra would not give her an ounce of space to condemn her and Peter in anyway, shape or form. For surely, if anything resulted (and she hoped it would not) from last nights invasion, Mara would be sure that it happened in the Tent on this Safari.

Petra refused to become Victim of this *'challenge'*.

She showered again, though she wondered how she could be the least bit unclean – even though deep down, she felt *DIRTY.*

The Mirror told her that there was a lot of Stress in that face. Deliberately she stretched her jaws and mouth until it represented a smile of sorts.

Petra had learned that long ago – Practice Smiling. You do not want to end up with an angry face like Mara or even Daddy. Mom at least tried to smile as often as she could.

Not Mara. Petra wondered if Mara thought it safer that way – looked more authoritative or something.

Grandad Peter was always smiling. The smiling Peter irked Mara though because she could not recognize what he was up too. She could not figure out why he is happy when he does not go to church. Sure, he goes to those 'meetings' in somebody's house somewhere; but that's not Church. And she was not the least interested. Her girlfriends were in Church.

By now, Petra had learned that though she might not be Blood, she and Grandad were alike in consulting often with their own,
Integrity InnerNet of LOVE. Few know of this avenue to get the Smile On!

Most are wrapped up in what they hear from the Podium, the internet, the media, and the Gossip Line behind the Masks.

Petra, in her need for Quiet, found the InnerNet much more reliable than any of those lines of communication. Too much manipulation and deception in them.

She was sure Grandad felt the same.

This morning, Petra automatically packed the few belongings she had back in her backpack before she left the bedroom. She would leave them in the Truck and decide later what to do.

She methodically stripped the sheets. Along with the towels and bathroom stuff, she placed them in the washer on Hot. Sanitize she thought. Mara could think what she wanted when she found them there.

But she *WOULD NOT BE GOING BACK IN THAT ROOM -EVER!*

Fortunately, Mara was seldom in the kitchen as she prepared her breakfast and left for College.

Grandad had supplied her with a small truck from the mine for transportation. 'Bokamosa Diamond' sparkled on the door panels.

Preface

Just in case you missed these details in Book One, here is a brief outline of what has gone before.

After the forgoing event, Petra asked Naomi and Grandad if she could sleep at Naomi's in the Gate House. They agreed noticing something had changed in Petra's cheery countenance.

Peter senior had sold the Diamond business and the Estate except for a few acreages kept for Naomi's family, for Sara and for Petra though now there was only Petra from that family.

Naomi is Peter's Forever Friend. Unexpectedly over 50 years earlier Peter came home from Duty to find himself already married to Mara – an Arranged Marriage to cover his father David's lust. Peter was the only child of David and Mayana Bokamosa that survived birth. Mayana died shortly after the arranged marriage of her son.

Peter had honored that marriage and the vows he did not make but were part of the license. Mara's mother and Mara had been taken off the Street by David Bokamosa to help with Estate Duties since his wife was unwell.

Peter sr. had given Petra the information and Gift from her Birth Father about a week before the previous event occurred. Mara considered both

Petra and Peter jr. illegitimate children – Peter of her blood, but Petra a stepchild.

Mara believed that Petra and Peter were engaged because of the gift Petra wore from her father. The 2 Peters and Petra played along with her game, knowing the Truth: but never anticipating the previous complications of the situation.

However, Mara makes a Huge Issue reporting the engagement and 'with child' to Petra's already stressed-out parents who have just buried their youngest daughter and granddaughter.

They send tickets for Petra's return to Canada; not to home, but to an isolated cabin – alone.

Prior to the next chapter, Grandad Peter had left 4 people at the Johannesburg Airport with a different plan for Petra than she thought was about to happen.

A more satisfactory plan than she could have imagined. Grandad was LOVE!

Chapter 5

Grandad Peter had been busy the past few years getting everything exactly right. No, he was not consulting much with family about business matters. He had learned it was better that way. He could keep LOVE in the plan and by-pass the greed and selfishness of some he would deal with later.

For the past 3 years he had been working on the plan, steadily making progress.

Yes, he had consulted Mara as to her choices for a Retirement Home. He had the scrapbook she had put together for him. He could have guessed most of it, but then she would have room to say she had no say in the matter and he wanted none of that.

He, Peter Bokamosa would come clean with no regrets when his life was over. Anyway, that was his plan when the business of closure started.

If Mara was happy, that increased his happy, though his happy was from a deep inner Source that needed no one else to source it. It came from his own InnerNet as his granddaughter identified the Source as.

However, there were a lot of folks in his life that he considered Family, and he wanted to make them all feel special. You can do that when you have the financial support to do so. When you know you do not need to hoard any of it and do not need most of it.

He was always thanking his Creator for favouring him so much. He was a Generous and Charitable Man of Integrity which no one could deny.

Yes, there were things he would have changed if he were given the chance to change at the time. No, life had not been Rose Blossoms – the thorns had pierced him deeply.

As he told Peter and Petra "adds a facet that sparkles to the beholder."

But the Creator had helped him through the rough spots and given him grace for all the journey this far. He did not want to mess up the final years. He would make the most of the years he had left. Maybe do some of the things he always wanted to do but had too many responsibilities to do.

Peter felt blessed in the way things all happened. He realized he could not have planned it better himself if he had tried concerning the sale of properties etc.

Even the events of the past few months, having Petra around to cheer him.

Peter his name sake was always a joy to him.

Maria was a beautiful and confident lady even though she had never married. She had conquered her fears. Maria had moved on in life.

He still had his lovely Naomi even though he had lost a dear friend in Bob. He would never forget all of Bob's labor and his being there for him when times got rough with Mara.

Bob who understood he loved Naomi no less than he ever did.

Bob who kept his Naomi safe from any harm. Bob who opened his home to Peter knowing that Peter and Naomi would have been married and he may have missed Naomi's Love if David Bokamosa had not

thrown in the hammer – had him married to Mara before he even came home.

He would never forget the joy of having so many times with them around the Bible and what it really meant; for introducing him to 'the home meetings' and all the friends he met along the way because of those meetings.

Maybe that is the one thing he would have done different. He would have said 'No' to his father's arrangement. But then he would never have known Bob if he married Naomi as they had planned.

So, in the long run, life had given him both plus Family. He could not ask for more.

His competitor in mining was a much younger man. Born Rich! He wanted to buy Bokamosa Diamonds. Who was Grandad to say No?

It all started happening in his favor 17 months after Mara decided it was time to stop working and enjoy her Estate Home.

The price was right. The terms were good. It was not all cash though. It included a property in the suburbs – in the very area that Mara indicated she would like to live. Now get this, Peter thought, 'the very house she pointed out to him when they went touring'.

How lucky is that!

So, the deal was made, and all things said and done over a three year period to complete by November 30.

Young Peter helped him move his office to the Office in the Gate House next to the Coach Storage area. It was not being used since Bob died, so why not!

In the process, he had trades men working on the House in the suburb to get it ready for the Gift at year end.

****

One day, he was having coffee with some of his acquaintances at the local café. A fellow he had grown up with asked if he ever thought of selling the Estate House? This fellow already knew that Peter had sub-divided portions for all who meant anything dear to him.

Grandad had waited until Petra visited to see if the Estate House Parcel might be something she would like to own. After a couple of months, and she had moved to Naomi's, he decided it would not work for her. She had an aversion to the house. He had not twigged in to just Why until just a few days ago when he and Naomi viewed the security camera rolls.

So, when this enquiry came, Grandad said "I have considered it. What is your interest?"

The fellow told him his son had been successful and was looking for a place back in the area.

"He knows your place. Seems he and David went to school together, and he asked me to ask you. He knows you are getting older and might want to move off."

The deal was made. Papers signed all online. Imagine that! Grandad could hardly believe how all this stuff flies these days.

Why Aircraft of any kind was new in his beginning days.

However, there was a hitch. This Bradley man wanted possession before the New Year. It put Peter into a bit of a rush, but somehow it could be managed.

Mara would not have to move much, as all the things she had requested in the scrapbook were already in the New Place.

And that is how things are for Peter Bokamosa!

– LOVE covers a lot.

Chapter 6

The plan that Peter Senior and Naomi had come up with in the short time they had, was revealed to Jamie in the Airport.

Once inside, Naomi asked Petra to look in her envelop to check on its contents. She had been so saddened, that she had not given her envelop another glance except to bring it along. Within the envelop, there was another envelop addressed to Jamie Gillette Parker in Grandad's large scrawl.

Within it was the Replacement. Yes, it was the original Cape Town Ticket. The Departure date on the Ticket out of Cape Town, was for January 6. Peter's tickets returned to Johannesburg on the 4th.

Briefly, Petra wondered whatever was she going to do in Cape Town by herself for 3 days?

Grandad had included a letter as well.

Dear Jamie,

I could see no reason for going along with Henri's plan. It was a rather ridiculous one. It made no sense to my old heart. I have decided to take things into my own hands, and I will assume all the blame that may be laid before you.

I have some business ends to tie up before the end of the year. However, I am using your extra ticket to Cape Town on January 2 to escort you back to Canada.

Naomi and I will be accompanying you back to Canada. You will not be alone right off the bat. I wanted to be sure you would be alright in your isolated place. I would not be able to sleep knowing the dangers of a 5-hour taxi ride either. Therefore, I have booked a flight for you to a smaller airport close to the cabin. Naomi and I have rooms near the Airport in Victoria.

You will be picked up by Willow or her son when you arrive at the Tofino Airport.

A few days later, we will use the Uber ticket to the cabin. Once we are rested, we will contact the Driver to pick us up and follow to the cabin. Give you time to settle in, and us time to rest Old Bodies. Give us a chance to see the scenery as well.

Your attacker will be in custody before long. And the rest, I will update you with when we meet again on January 2.

Enjoy your holiday without fear.
We all LOVE you Dearly.

Sincerely,
Peter Bokamosa sr.

Grandad went home from the Airport to complete the Business he had set about a week earlier with the help of Naomi, Maria, and Peter.

Petra would see Grandad again in just over a week. Her heart skipped a beat as he gave her a hug and said, "See you the evening of January 2." She did not wish to rush time, but she did value Grandad Peter's presence and wisdom.

Chapter 7

"Naomi, what shall I tell you? Grandad told me I must, and I know he is a wise man."

"Maybe I can start this conversation for you Petra. When was the first time you remember being sexually touched?"

"Sometimes pain persists out of empathy
rather than tissue damage. Tissue
heals, but nerves remember."

"Having to go back to Canada, this past week I have been remembering a lot I do not want to go back to. Though it will be lonely after having all your company, the Cabin is likely a Blessing."

"Naomi I am going to use names. I do not have to call someone 'Dad' any more that is not my Dad. I will never stop calling Grandad, 'Grandad' because he has never stopped loving me. I have no occasion where forgiveness is necessary with him. HE IS LOVE."

"Okay! I wonder if there was ever a time that Henri did not touch us girls in questionable ways? I do not wish to make him criminal. I believe it is more that he did not recognize that 'the nerves remember', like you just said.

"One of my first memories is of having a diaper change and giggling because Henri was tickling my genitalia. I do not think it happened as a regular thing. If it did, I probably would not remember it as vividly."

"About twice a year, Henri goes berserk! I mean literally Naomi. I do not know how Mom has put up with him this long. I think he knows he does too because sometimes he will leave for a day or two. I don't know where he goes, but maybe where 'weir wolves' go. That might sound like I am joking, but that is how he is."

"I know he is on a lot of medications and I often wondered if it was when they changed something for 'his nerves'?" In 'Prozac Panacea or Pandora?' Ann Blake Tracy says that stuff like that can happen – the change or going off the drug can make them act out."

"Did you ever see him in one of those when he was growing up?"

"Unfortunately, yes."

"Do you want me to call you Jamie too? I noticed Grandad started calling you that."

"That would be a kindness Naomi!"

"Jamie you are!"

"Yes, Jamie it often happened when they changed his medication. OR later I came to understand it happened regularly with the dark of the moon – New Moon phase especially in winter months."

"It was a medication switch about two days before Peter was conceived."

"That helps to know. When these spells happen, it exhausts mother. First night she seems to endure his sexual demands. Then she will often come sleep with one of us girls the next couple of nights until he settles down again."

"In later years, Mom said that Sara is too restless in bed, so she would mostly sleep with me. Where Mom was not, after we moved to Canada, he came to the other quiet enough that Mom was not aware. If she was, she pretended not to notice or know."

"He managed to do a lot of touching with me. I was a fighter from a young age. No, I did not make noise because I did not want to waken Mom. I would not let him in. Yes, I got spanked and yanked, but I knew it was not right – like you said, my nerves knew. I also heard a lot about 'I'll fix that whole in your head yet, you illegitimate child'. Sad but true."

"Though sometimes I was exhausted, and he pumped between my legs just above my knees. I hated the Yuk in my bed. I stripped my sheets as soon as he left and cry myself to sleep. I probably got off easy."

"Sara was a different case – she told me once when she was about 13, that if I would give in, he would make me feel good. I could not allow myself to do that. And of course, I had Mom in bed with me way more than she did by then."

"We girls were supplied with Birth Control Pills the minute it was thought we might be starting our period. "To regulate our Period" we were told. Mine was clockwork since day 1 so why would I need to take them? I saw too many pills being pushed at our house."

"My Integrity-InnerNet told me that was garbage, and I would cause myself health problems later if I took the Pill. So other than the first week, I never took them. Sara took mine and supplied one of her classroom friends."

"Besides, I thought Why am I taking these pills when I have no intention of going to bed with a boy until I am married? So, I didn't."

"Guess it would have been a good idea 3 weeks ago. How would I have guessed?"

"Anyway, to clear the air, Petri and I were awfully close on Grad weekend. You do not spend nearly 60 hours with someone you love without getting touchy."

"However, we were studying ACIM together and what LOVE really is. We both want to give our Virginity to the one we marry. We both understand what Integrity means to us as a virtue. Really, Naomi humans can control urges if they listen to their InnerNet instead of all the songs that sound like sex."

"So, there was nothing we did that could have conceived. And you know that Peter and I are more like cousins – best friends than intimate. That is why it really bugged me when Mara kept insisting that I was pregnant."

"With Child" Naomi joked.

"Right! As if that makes it sound better."

"Naomi, I have gathered that you and Grandad would have married if his father had not had him married off to Mara unexpectedly. Naomi, you do not have to answer my question if you choose not to, but did you and Grandad have intercourse at anytime? I do not wish to embarrass you, so don't answer if it makes you uncomfortable."

"Jamie, that is not hard to answer. Grandad has full respect for me. Always has had. We first started dating when I was 15 and he about 17. From the beginning, he told me that if ever he should get out of line, to let him know."

"Our first dates were going to Church meetings together. He liked my modesty in appearance, and I guess the Spirit of my life essence. He wanted to know more about what I believed. As you know, we still go to those meetings together. We are both thankful for you having joined us since you came too."

"That being said, nearly sixty years having passed, no, our relationship did not go that far, and I can confidently say it will not as long as he is married to a wife. I will not hinder his vows to Mara, though it is not much of a relationship anymore."

"Really it never was. Peter is a good man, and he is also a Peace Maker. He has done his best in honoring vows he was forced to make. Had we understood the deceptions it was a cover for, we would likely have married before he left on duty. But that is enough of our dynamics. You have your answer. Now continue your story please."

"Thank you, Naomi! Reassuring that relationships can be had without sex included. I think that is the Grad Gift Petri gave me – The confidence that you can be with someone you love without making it a sex scene. That is respect as I see it."

"When we came back from the Safari weekend, I was tired. I felt gritty from the sand dust and knew I required a shower. A quick one and wrapped the towel around me. As hot as it was, covers were not a requirement. Really, I have no idea if I locked my door or even shut it."

"You had. It was locked. Grandad and I watched the security camera footage together. The gardener unlocked it with a nail."

"Was I bad Naomi? Do you think it was my fault? Like that I wanted him to do it to me?"

"No child. You were innocent. Yes, we could see the struggle to try and move. I know that FROZEN phase when I see it. The thing more concerning to me, is how the person deals with it afterward. What did you do after?"

"I got myself to the bathroom and washed a lot. Cried. Washed some more and then soaked in the tub for awhile. I made a bed on the bathroom floor and loaded up with heavy PJs. No chance of getting into those. I could hear him laughing hideously through the walls. I threw up. Finally, I slept on the cool floor."

"Naomi have you ever heard of 'Ho'oponopono'? it is a Hawaiian prayer practice. I used it to help me deal with Henri, so I began saying it that night. I also like to finish by saying 'Father forgive them, they know not what they do.' Like Jesus did."

"The next night, I asked to stay at your house. I could not bear to sleep there again. That morning I packed my Backpack and put it in my truck. I did not care that Mara would have more to say. Or even that it might hurt Grandad. I wanted out of there. That morning I had no idea where I would move to either."

"But then when I missed my period that should have come less than two weeks later, the whole thing started to roll my stomach. It would be something to be pregnant with a child from someone you really admired, like Peter or even Petri, but this creepy stranger?"

"Yuk! It is obvious I do not see what Mara sees in him."

This was the conversation as the Plane flew them to Cape Town for the holiday Peter II had planned for them. And maybe a chance meeting with Marabella's Family. At least Petra could have a drive-by her Great-Grandparent's place and maybe see the Parking Pad at the back where her grandad parked the Bus.

"Did you know Peter has investigated who the Gardener is?
Peter has been very suspicious that he is not a Horticulturist as he claims. He likely attended the Club because it is attended by Wealthy Women like Mara."

"Peter and Maria helped Grandad put a movie of his findings together along with the security camera footage. Very convincing, but Grandad is extremely cautious that no flags are raised before the arrest can happen. We will be hearing from Grandad in a few days."

"Naomi, I am feeling better already knowing that I am not condemned in your family's eyes. I love you all so much. You all have been my saving grace these past few months."

"And to know that I have a Daddy who loves me even though he has never seen me and did not know I happened." Jamie fingered the ring on her middle finger. She would love to share this part with her Mother. But how would it upset Henri's low esteem?

What did it matter? Henri and Mara needed to be put in a bag and shaken. Maybe it would *"Fix the Hole in their Heads."*

Would they never recognize the Gems they have in their lives that 'cover a multitude of sin with their LOVE?'

The flight was about halfway. They both knew they required a little shut eye, if not sleep.

Chapter 8

The year before, Peter Bokamosa had sub-divided the place so that Naomi's Family would have property and Naomi would not be without a home should she outlive him. He knew Mara too well.

The month before, he did a lot of Banking and Legal work. His competitor bought him out. He resisted for a long time. Now he understood in his bones, that even though Peter and Petra were interested in Diamonds, they did not need it cluttering their lives.

Bokamosa Diamond would be incorporated into Ashcroft Diamond Inc. the completion being December 1st.

Naomi's family knew. Mara did not. The mines had never had her name attached to them. Did she even care if she could live in luxury?

The proceeds were being divided among his 'Family' as fairly as he could. He had quizzed Mara a bit over three years ago to see if she appreciated living on the Estate, or would she rather live in the Suburbs? She always said in Town and told him how she would decorate it. Obviously not a masculine environment.

A couple of times he had taken her for a drive on a Sunday afternoon to get a sense of her likings and the area she would like to be in. If she was honest, she was getting the place she had pointed out. Nothing over the top, but elegant. Peter took possession of it for her, in her name, nearly 3 years earlier. He planned to surprise her as a Yearend Gift.

As for himself, he felt like the main estate was too much for him. He had two other 10-acre plots divided when he did the Gate House. One for Peter jr. and one for Maria. They could build, do whatever they wanted with it. Sell it if they wished.

A Gift was given with no strings attached.

He considered Petra in the property as well. Maybe the main house? He was waiting until she was here a year or two to see how she felt about the idea. Now he knew it was not an idea he even wanted to enter her mind. He had something else in mind now. That is why the push this week to get things aligned with his integrity.

He had not yet dealt with the gardener and Mara on the case. BUT he had a case as sure as anything. He did not want to get involved in court proceedings. He did not want Petra to go through that repulsive process that would really embed the bad in her nervous system.

Instead, he would find out who this Dr. Gardener really was and fire him. The choice would be Mara's as to whether the gardener was going with her or not.

At any rate, Separation Proceedings were being lined up. Never did he believe he would be doing this. But there needed to be a Separation Settlement so that she was looked after but would have no say in the rest of the finances, or even his life for that matter.

However, how long can a man live with all the deception in his house? Generations of it.

Again, he was thankful for the comfort Naomi's family brought to him even though he could not be married to her. Oh, how he loved Bob as well when he met him. An Honest Man! He was also glad that Bob and

Naomi's LOVE could include him as they did. He could not think of a better person for Naomi since their betrothal could not happen due to his father's arrangement. He just shook his head to think of his father's scheme even after over 50 years.

To his amazement he would not have to fire the Gardener. Mara would have no choice in keeping or letting him go. There was plenty of evidence and Authorities involved now that the man would be revealed.

Peter had been a great help to him learning all this new age technology. If it were not for that boy, he had to concede he would be pretty much an old man.

The week after they had visited the mine office, the two Peters had moved Grandad's office and personal belonging into the lower-level office at the Gate House. It was at the bottom of the stairs to the left, whereas the door to the garage part was to the right.

He was grateful for the help and happy with the arrangement. The office had not been used since Bob's stroke, so a little dusting was all it needed. It included a small Bachelor Suite tucked behind the office. An Ideal place for Peter's retirement.

He would have used the suite for his hang out if Mara did not have that gardener. Now he knew he should have; but then the rascal would likely have come in some other way.

And now he was thankful his Creator took it into hand and sold the Estate House and property for him. With so much speeding his alignment up, his mind was a bit weary.

He still had the hardest part to address.

Present the evidence to Mara in Dr. Gardener's presence. He would wait until after supper. He would endure the small talk since Gardener was at the table as well. It was Christmas Eve, and Mara was all cheerful about going to church. But this time, Peter Bokamosa stood his ground.

Mara saw he was determined – maybe he was not a weak man after all. Maybe he had given in to her just to keep her happy. Whatever, he seemed to have a Big Plan he would not allow her to tamper with. Church or no church!

First, Peter took them for a drive. He drove up to the house he had Renovated for Mara. The lights were on, and the yard was decorated in the manner Mara generally decorated at the Estate.

He was not dumb. He had taken note of the colors she stated, the type of furnishings and all. Before Gardener had come into their lives, he would ask her for pictures of things she liked.

About 3 years ago, he had her fix an album with the things she thought were important in a house. Her retirement house.

He had a professional designer decorate it over the past 2 years in preparation for this day.

He was not exactly happy having Gardener along, but he needed to make things as unsuspecting as possible for later. He stopped and Mara just looked with her mouth in awe!

"Well, shall we look in? I have a key" he said as he opened his car door.

No, there is no snow in Johannesburg this time of year. However, Grandad had wanted this incredibly special for Mara. Of course, all these special things were added to the plan prior to knowing Gardener existed. He allowed them anyway. The grass was covered with 'spray snow'. The trees had a layer of thin quilt batting to make them look snow covered.

Grandad went ahead and unlocked the door.

Mara could hardly believe her eyes! And there on the front hall table was the Book of Dreams he had asked her to make between 3-5 years ago. She remembered clearly.

She had to admit – This man is genuine, and I did not get it!

And they were not in church tonight.

Chapter 9

Second, Peter took them back to the Gatehouse Office and sat
them down comfortably. He told them that the place was subdivided
and sold. If she would package her personal belongings, and the things
she wished to take with her, he had a moving company coming to pick
them up on the twenty-seventh. The other folks had a possession date of
January 1 and he wanted time for the Cleaning and Estate Eliminators
to do their work.

He apologized for cramming the time. Explained how their behavior
around Petra had thrown him off with having to deal with other details.

He assured them that knowing everything was prepared at the other
end, there would not be all that much packing to do. So, he was sure she
could do it in the time allotted – after all, she did have this Gardener
fellow to help her if she did not kick him out before hand.

He told them that he divided up the estate finances and that besides her
new home, she had plenty to finish her days with.

He also stated firmly that she was not to be Gossiping about any of this
or complaining as to how he chose to divide it up. Seeing the mess, she
had made for their granddaughter, she needed to count herself lucky.

He asked her a question: "Mara did you ever wonder why Petra started sleeping away from the Estate House? Were you happy to have the house to yourself for the convenience of your Guest, Mr. Rami Raju?

Mara said she had no idea of who he was talking about, and had he gone completely mad?

He could see that Mr. Raju was getting extremely uncomfortable. The exact reaction he was hoping to see. Hoping the man had conscience. With the help of a Private Investigator over the past several months, Grandad had been tracing this Professor Gardener. From the get-go, he was not comfortable that he was who he said he was, and who Mara believed him to be.

With the 'Petra event' he intensified the search for identity. Only Naomi knew what he was up to. Only after they remembered the security cameras, were they able to find some conclusive evidence.

With Peter and Maria's help over the past week, they were able to pull enough off the internet and now the surveillance cameras to have the evidence that they might just have a serial sex offender on their hands.

There was enough evidence to nail this man now. Grandad's Investigator had been there as a 'home inspector' to take Fingerprints one day. The police were involved.

Things were drawing to the point of arrest. And then it was time for Grandad's BOMB.

And now, he said, "I have a movie I would like you to watch together. It will be easy to identify the actors."

He had Peter help him put up a movie screen and teach him how to run the projector. He wanted the production as large as life so that there could be no denials. Included were previous charges. Prison Terms. Countries and aliases, he had lived in and used.

"Shall we roll?" said Grandad.

There were a few face shots of the man wanted. There were a few news items – just enough for Mara to recognize her Guest.

Peter heard the vehicles quietly drive up.

The movie continued now with the Hall camera – the one that had both the bedroom Petra had been in and the door to the suite. The camera revealed it was not the first time Rami had entered the bedroom.

Evidence was that Rami had used a nail to unlock Petra's door. He had not bothered to shut the door after himself, which was not in his favor at this point. The camera was low enough that it showed the complete movie on the bed.

Rami was really wiggling now. Peter was expecting him to bolt at any moment.

All Mara could keep saying was "Unbelievable! Unbelievable!" her eyes riveted to the screen.

And then came Rami walking toward the camera on his exit, looking right at the Camera with a Big Grin to stand there and stick his tongue out at the camera – as if to say, 'sure fooled you since I flipped your switch'!

Apparently, he had turned the breaker to the security off for the house the day he came. He did not know there was a 'bypass' on Grandad's office computer that never allowed the cameras to be turned off.

Rami knew he had played the fool carelessly now. He bolted to the door only to be caught by two Policemen waiting for his exit. Handcuffed, they took him to his suite to pick up his identification and necessities. One officer noticed the computer was on with camera screens like at the desk of hotels.

They asked Grandad if they could do a search of the house. Sure enough, they found cameras in each bathroom including Mara's personal dressing room and Petra's bathroom above the tub that focused on the mirror. He had suggested to Mara that full length mirrors on the door, opposite the vanity mirror would be a good idea 'so she could see the back of her head when doing her hair etc. Of course, it would be nice to have in their Guestroom Bath as well.'

Little would anyone know there was an ulterior motive. *No wonder Petra heard the hideous laughter – he was watching her sob, vomit and try to cleanse away the filth she felt.*

There was a camera aimed at Petra's bed. He knew exactly when to enter.

The Police seized the computer and asked if they could come back the next day and dismantle the cameras that Rami had planted – very tiny cameras.

Peter took a shaken Mara back to the house. Smitten she knew she had but one choice. Pack her belonging and be ready for the move on December 27.

Caught in her own trap, she began to weep recognizing the pain she had caused Peter and Petra just to selfishly cover her own ignorance and hidden secrets.

Recognizing the pain, she had caused this man Peter who had been true to her all these years, even though she could not control her own need for love in the form of sexual contact with more than one man.

She knew she needed Professional help to take off the Mask she had been covering a multitude of sin with. No. It was not love at all. But she felt like she was too old for the kind of help she required. Like an alcoholic or a smoking habit, Mara recognized she had a habit that was too painful to open about even to herself. And how could she deal with her friends finding out? *My Peter's Gift* was enough to cover the past for anyone else to know.

Here in her presence was a man of LOVE. A man who had never met her until the day that David Bokamosa Sr. had them married to cover his own sin with her. She had let him down.

She had let his only child die when he wanted to take her to the Mayo Hospital for more advanced treatment.

She had let him slip through her fingers in the Name of Church – slip from her for a moments pleasure with a criminal.

Clarity came too late.

Chapter 10

Peter was not a money man. It had never been important to him. He had learned from his father's example of what he did not want to be around money.

"Good People invest money in Good Projects.
Bad People use money for hidden agendas."

However, right now he was glad he had a bit of it. How else do you speed things up so you can get on with the important things in life. No; it was not bribery; it was Rewarding Good Behavior on the behalf of all it concerned.

He wanted to be on that Plane for Cape Town on January 2. He wanted a couple nights of good sleep, before the long overseas flight. He knew at his age; he needed more rest time than youngsters do. Still there was a lot to accomplish as he would not return until March 2nd – unless Petra returned from Cape Town and change his mind.

He had given it a lot of consideration as to who he should send on this trip. Finally, he knew he required standing behind his own tampering with plans. He would bare the blame for the changes he made, not Jamie. And besides that, he had a thing or two he wanted to straighten out with Henri and Marabella.

Huh! If they will even let him into their busy lives. How twisted families can become, especially when they really are not families, but a bunch of mixed-up relationships with very little True LOVE.

Look at Mara – bearing two of his own father's children. So, confused that she would not allow him to take sweet little Lucy to America for medical attention lest he not bring her back. No one said Mara was not going along, but Mara herself since she did not trust flying.

Well, we lost Lucy anyway. Maybe she was better off. She missed all the fighting and the assaults by brothers and strangers.

Bless God for taking her so innocently.

Mr. Raju was out of the way. He knew he could not back up the time, but oh how he wished he had said No to his presence on the Estate the day he became suspicious of his hidden identity.

Mara's van would arrive in the morning to move her stuff. She had enough women folk oohing and awing over her new digs, that he was not required to be there to unpack.

Two people in new digs – He wondered how the gardener was feeling in his Striped Pajamas? And even though he made his own joke of it, Peter felt sorry for people – being their own worst enemy.

He would move what he required over to Naomi's before he left. He had a list of things each one could use as the Estate Transitionary Company moved in to clean up.

He still had to meet with the lawyer at land titles on the 31$^{st.}$

Then he would be a FREE MAN!

He was wondering how Free Mara was feeling. How Free her gardener was feeling?

He would accompany Jamie to the Cabin if she had not decided to stay in Africa. By the time they would arrive, Henri and Marabella would be back home he was sure.

However, it was probably best that they go to the Cabin first and get rested up. No point challenging a Den of Lions ill equipped. Jamie could take them with her vehicle back to the city once they were rested.

His excitement about the Trip with Naomi was setting in. His idea was to get them a suite near Victoria Airport for a few nights so that they could get rested. Then they would take the Uber Ride to the Cabin to meet up with Jamie again.

He chuckled to himself as he thought of her new name. He hoped she liked it as much as he did or maybe as much as her Birth Daddy did? It suited her a lot more than Petra did.

Peter wanted to make sure he knew how Henri and Marabella were doing – their situation before he booked a flight to Rochester. Might as well see his friend Dr. Benjamin Parker while he was on that side. And show his Naomi some more of the World.

And so, it was!

Chapter 11

Cape Town was in an enjoyable Festive spirit. A little noisy for Petra's liking, but still she was in enjoyable company that understood the True Christ Story. She did not want to miss anything or have any preconceived ideas as to how and what should be.

She simply would not Tarnish the Joy of the Moment with the 'what ifs' of the future, and probably there would be lots of them.

Each day they visited a new area of the city or took an excursion into the surrounding country. There was a lot of fun and laughter. Petra noticed that these 3 did not need alcoholic drinks to be happy.

They did use Essential Oils every morning on their bodies to keep their immune system boosted. She had grown fond of the scents being around Naomi's house. Maybe they were 'high on Scent' instead. This was not synthetic fragrance, but Nature – her style. No matter. Petra was content being in their company and following along.

One day, they took a trip out to the area that Marabella's grandparents once lived. Petra had no idea that they would even be alive yet. They would be old for sure.

As they slowed to view the address, they noticed the Motorhome and parking pad still in good condition. Obviously, someone still cared for the place. As they came to the front, the gate was open, so they drove in. As they drove by the wrought iron gate, the Gold lettering still sparkled 'Karabo'.

"Would you like to go to the door Petra? The worst they can do is throw us out."

Curious, Petra opened her door and stepped out onto the red brick drive and walk to the front door. Hesitantly she lifted the Knocker. A dog barked from within. She heard shuffling noises from within.

Soon a lady about Naomi's age came to the door. She first squinted at Petra standing there. Petra was not sure what to say, or what would happen next. It seemed she was tongue tied as to what to say.

The woman said, "Are you for real?"

Immediately she scooped Petra into a warm embrace – completely surprising her with the response.

Then the woman, about her same size, held her back by the shoulders and said, "Petra I can hardly take this in girl! Your school photos have arrived every year with Marabella's newsy letter to her Grandparents, my parents. I only wished that some year she would bring you girls to visit us. I know it was a long way to come. That was her choosing."

"What brings you back?" she asked as she spotted the vehicle and others with Petra. She waved her arm to invite them all in.

"This is worth investing the rest of the day in. My folks will be so happy to see their Great Granddaughter! From your features, you must be Petra, the oldest."

This was happening about December 28.

So Karabo must have been her grandmother's maiden name. I do remember mother saying her parents never took wedding vows. And that they were nomadic as she referred to them. Hippy was likely more accurate.

Karol Karabo took them around back to the Sun Porch to meet her folks – Dr. Carl Karabo and Mini Karabo. Great Grandad was all of 99. He was born New Years Eve, well actually at the stroke of midnight but not considered the New Year yet.

Because he was turning 100 this year on December 31, the family were to gather for a Festive occasion. They would be so happy if Petra and her other family were to join them and meet cousins, uncles and aunts and you name it.

Carl was still of active mind, but fragile in body. He was in a Zero Recliner with a blanket around him. He did not seem to retain body heat anymore.

Mini was a bubbly lady. Slightly dementia but still a very cheerful lady – excited about the visitors and what they could do for them to make them feel comfortable. She was a bit demanding of Karol, but Karol did not seem to mind. She simply took it all in stride.

Once they all were seated, Karol brought out a large pitcher of Iced Tea – a flavor Petra never tasted before; slightly fermented and fizzy. During conversation, they found out it was Kombucha, a fermented tea drink that was full of natural enzymes for wellness.

Petra could hardly believe the Love these relatives related to her. Made her wonder whatever was it that Marabella wanted '*to leave dead lions buried*'? But then Petra had not met her father either; or any of the other siblings for that matter. It was only Grandma Karabo and Great Grand Parents yet.

Her curiosity was stirred again and a huge mountain of gratitude to grandad Peter for making it possible for her to enjoy these weeks with relatives.

Yes, Petra got a tour of the bus. It was kept up and cleaned as a Guest House when family were around.

Karol lived in the house with her folks as a constant caregiver. Karl could still walk with support and do most things for himself. He was almost as gentle and sweet as Grandad Peter.

Mini was a bit of a challenge as she did not realize that her mind was smaller than her desire to serve and keep things in order.

Amazing to Petra, but Karol and Naomi recognized that they followed the same Way of Faith – they recognized the same gentle Spirit if not the same Hymn Book in the music area.

Karol told Naomi that she had been a rebel when she left home and aligned with Marabella's father to raise their children. She took responsibility for the family dynamics she created for her children and the mess her relationship finally ended up in.

She found out that Gerry Kran was not exactly the right kind of father she should have chosen for her children; especially for her two daughters.

After moving home to look after her parents, she returned to enjoy what they had enjoyed all their lives. What Peace it had returned to her.

Ah! Petra wondered if Marabella had been running away from The Faith by going to the other side of the continent as well.

Yes, no doubt running away from a man like Henri to complete the lesson with a man of similar traits. Petra had learned in the courses she was taking that we often marry someone just like the parent we *'had unfinished business'* with, unless we challenge our emotions and let that classroom go.

All in all, it was a good day. And Yes, they would return in a couple of days for the 100th Birthday Party. Surely it would be as Grand as Mara's, only on the other side of the continent and with people Who LOVE.

This in, and of itself was a wonderful Surprise and Gift from Peter jr.! She fell into bed a weary mind that night but full of soul joy to find out how easy it was to get to know these folks with whom she shared a blood line through her mother, Marabella.

Life is Good after all!

Chapter 12

Petra is coming through strongly this morning. I shall let her take over.

Leaving Africa was not an easy decision. All these family members that honored my existence. All the support of so many, and my child would be loved by them all no matter who or what he looked like. Interesting that I should be calling the fetus 'him' already! Maybe like my father Benjamin says, "we Sioux know things we don't know."

I was certainly surprised to see so many of my mother's family at the airport in Cape Town this morning as the 3 of us were about to pass through security and fly away. How could Marabella think of these people as '*dead lions*'? They were very full of LOVE as far as I could see.

Of course, I did not meet Gerry Kran. Apparently, he was too good at 'Raising a Family from Scratch' as his book writing, scientific experiments, and Workshops were about. Maybe he 'scratched' one too many times, and Grandma Karol Karabo along with her parents help sent him packing to scratch for himself.

Of course, that was about the time my mother entered Residency and was on her own. Karol, my Karabo Grandmother understood things were going on with him '*undercover*' that she could no longer condone or hide from. Guess those are '*the leave dead lions buried*' my mother wished to have no part of.

But did she hold her mother responsible for what her father did? I realized I may never know, and it really did not matter now. But perhaps I was doing the same. My own grief over the fact that I would not seeing Sara 'in body' once I got back to Canada, had thrown a few darts at my mother, Marabella in this regard as well. Maybe I though that Mom could have saved us girls from Henri.

Poor Mom! I truly feel for her differently now that I have let go of those feelings and met 'the good side' of her background. **Mom *Is* the Good Side of my growing up**.

I have since learned that *'we often get into a relationship with a person like the parent we have unfinished business with'*.

Perhaps the Same Classroom with a different Teacher. Perhaps Marabella is living her criticism for her own mother for not pulling out sooner. I shall do my best to live my NOW in a way that does not carry garbage into my tiny Peter.

I got sidetracked there in remembrance of these lovely people. So back to the Canada journey about to begin.

I say 3 because Grandad Peter and Naomi are accompanying me back to Victoria. I will continue to the cabin on a connecting flight to Tofino as they rest up in Victoria. I hope it is not to overcast so they can see the splendor of the mountains. I will expect them up at the Cabin in a few days via the Uber I was supposed to be traveling on. Dear Grandad arranged the short flight so I could get settled; and they could see some of the Island once they are rested and in good order again.

At least this way, it will give me time to clean and get the furniture where I am comforted by it. I can have some time to go through boxes and see what all was sent with the clutter clearing of their daughters' stuff. And I would not be at all surprised to find that most of Sara's furniture and belongings are there too. Why sort when you can delegate to someone else? Henri style.

I have a lot of time to think today, as I journey toward a new life. I had started to really settle into South Africa once I moved to the Gate House. Even after I found myself pregnant, I knew I had a ton of support there and could move on in life just as Maria did some 30 years before.

I knew that Grandad Peter had subdivided a piece of property in my name. No, I did not have funds to build on it, but that did not bother me in the least. I knew once I honored my Talents the money would follow.

Then the abrupt change in plans that I wonder how I created. What am I desiring that this experience will give me? All things that I shall challenge in the quiet of my heart once we get into the air and level out. For now, I must watch out the window to keep my stomach under control. This apparently is a part of the first trimester of being pregnant.

Peter and Naomi have seats in 1st Class. I am at the back of the plane. I downloaded the Happiness frequency 9 hour recording to my phone so that I can listen and relax on the way home – well to what will be my home for at least a few months.

Time will tell whether I stay in a lonely place or move on my own somewhere. And that is a lie too. I am not alone. I have this little man growing inside of me. I will do everything possible to give him the best possible chance at life. I shudder to think of who his sire is. He does not need to know.

"I am sorry.
Please forgive me.
Thank you.
I love you."

Many times, on that flight I recited those words. Eventually they were not just words but LOVE flowing toward the little man within. And then I wonder if I am just teasing myself in thinking it is a boy when a girl could arrive?

Up to getting on the plane for Canada, I was in denial. I did not want to acknowledge that I could be pregnant with the child of a serial sex offender.

To be honest I did not wish to acknowledge I was pregnant with any one's child. I was looking for Freedom *not responsibility.*

It happened Girl. Get used to it. I had to do a lot of self talking to condition myself to give this fetus a chance in life. I sincerely hope my reluctance and rejection has not damage the emotions of the child in any way.

I made up my mind right then and there. I started calling the tiny being within Peter. I could always change to Petal if at some point it was discovered as a girl.

We began our communication over the South Atlantic. (really, via New York is the long way home. Someone was not thinking. Must have been a cheap flight.)

I looked down at the clouds below with tiny holes to see the ocean occasionally. I told Peter about all his wonderful relatives and their deep Faith.

I got an Epiphany and thought "Peter I know you are only 5-weeks, but do you have ears yet? I wonder if you enjoyed the Beautiful Singing in Harmony at your Great-Great-Grandad's 100th Birthday? I trust that you did. It made me happy too."

"We can be glad that Great-Grandad Peter and Naomi are coming to Canada with us. I know they already LOVE you."

I am now placing my hands on my belly in hopes that Peter feels like he is being held. It has taken me these weeks to adjust and accept that I am carrying a baby. My study now will be all about how this little thing progresses and what the best ways are to nurture in the womb.

Having taken the courses I did in Africa it was interesting to be introduced to the concepts of what emotional development takes place in the womb. As soon as I get settled at the Cabin and have internet hooked up, I shall see if I can get online courses to further the Arts and Sociology part of what I have already started.

Then I remember the cabin does not have a Power Source or even running water. No matter. I am not going to let the lacks spoil this present moment when I have time to get my mind wrapped around the fact that Peter and I will not always be one body.

I remember enough about the Cabin that I start to see the rooms in my mind and visualize the space and where the furniture that is there is, and where the furniture I believe was mine that was likely shipped there could go. Of course, once we are there maybe it will not fit as imagined; but at least we have a start.

All the travel time gives me a lot of time to think. I am determined to be Positive and keep LOVE in my life from above the love of humans.

And so, I shall look back on this time and wonder *'how many times did I Ho'oponopono about all of this? My own traumas; my Marabella traumas; Sara's traumas; and maybe even Henri's now that I understand Mara's background.*

And maybe even the traumatic heart ache Peter sr. and Naomi felt with their own wedding plans and life together being cancelled by a lusting and greedy parent covering his own sin.

Yes, it would not have been easy for either Naomi or Grandad. Oh, how I love their positive influence on my life in the past few months!'

In New York I met up with Grandad and Naomi. We had a nutritious lunch in the airport – well, as nutritious as you can get in an airport.

Again, they were up front and I further back. As we loaded, the Steward came back and asked if I would like to move to 1ˢᵗ Class. They were overbooked and required the seat for a young passenger to sit closer to their family.

Thankfully, I was right across from my relatives. Actually, Grandad chose to sit in the single seat so that I could sit by Naomi which suited me fine. I needed her ear for awhile. She seemed willing to listen.

Naomi quoted Thoreau:

> "The price of anything is the amount
> of life you exchange for it."

I had already started to realize this from within in the past few hours of flight. I was not willing to hang on to the trauma that presented me with tiny Peter. I learned a New Way of Life.

Living is not about Will Power to do what is required. Will Force takes a lot of energy to keep the battery charged.

Living from Curiosity as the Observer is much more fun and Energizes itself. This is The Child Way except that the Child has yet to learn the Power of Observation.

Naomi confirmed a lot of Beliefs that were good. I decided I could think about and build on Beliefs that set me Free Emotionally. She told me I did not have to accept Tiny Peter's siring as it was. I could create the Story that made life easier for both he and me. Forgiveness is an amazing antidote.

I started right then and there to drop the horror of that weary night and took my focus to Petri and the kindness he was to me graduation weekend. After all they did look similar and of the same nationality though this man was probably 20 or even 30 years older than Petri. Maybe his hard and remorseful life had aged him beyond years.

I knew the ability to be the Observer was powerful. I knew but did not practice observation up until this point. Now I was rehearsing in my mind many different possibilities of what <u>my Compelling Future</u> might hold. Like I was at the 'Y' in the road except that it had multiple branching. Which would I take? I knew it was too easy to get caught in the trap of self-pity or martyritis. I wanted neither. Yes, life as a young mother would have challenges. I told myself I am strong. As my father Ben told me: "With Christ we are enough."

My thoughts go temporarily to what life might have been like had he and Marabella continued their Love Life. To what good would that train of thought lead? It would only make me angry at having had to endure the *Henri Moments*.

One thing is for certain – I want to meet Dr. Benjamin Parker. Grandad and Naomi are traveling that way when they leave the Island. Maybe I should go with them?

No, I will not go now. I will go when Peter is old enough to enjoy travel. Just maybe Dr. Ben will come and visit us on the Island, at the Cabin. I will HOLD that one! And that is what I mentioned to Naomi as well.

We arrive in Vancouver and then on to Victoria. This must have been a cheap flight to have come from this direction. I have 2 hours in Victoria for which I am thankful. It is time enough to see Grandad and Naomi to their rooms and know that they are safe. Then back to the Terminal and on to Tofino.

By the time I am unloaded and into the car, it is who knows what hour. I have lost track of time, or even what day it is. Peter and Naomi must be very weary for their age.

Joey met me. He knew who he was looking for by a photo Willow gave him. I did not know who to look for at all except that I understood he had a speech impediment. The result of brain injury in an accident when he was in his teens.

It was a short ride, and we were at the cabin. Willow had a gas light lit. She gave me a very warm hug and then just as warm a Mug of Homemade Chicken Soup. I did not feel hungry. A bed seemed more appealing to my weary body and mind than food. However, the aroma of the soup stirred my soul to think of the LOVE in all this woman's kindness toward a stranger. She did not even know me, a tired and confused young woman.

She had a warm tub of water ready for me to dip into with the exotic fragrance of Rose.

Realize that the water had to be brought from the spring and heated for this luxury. Oh, how good it felt to be just a tiny bit pampered in the middle of mid-night. My head was aching from being awake or partially sleeping for over 48 hours. But finally, here I was – HOME where LOVE Dwells!

The Cabin was warm and relatively tidy. Boxes were piled high in one corner. Furniture was sort of placed in appropriate rooms. I had room to move. Willow showed me the indoor biffy to use for nights until I was familiar with the walk to the outhouse.

She slipped away with Joey and I was alone – "Oh, sorry tiny Peter, I guess We are Alone."

My head was full of motor noises and many other noises. Yet, I fell asleep quickly.

When I awakened, it was so quiet. The sun was in the western sky – I could not believe I had slept for 14 hours straight.

Thankful for the biffy Willow pointed out. I pulled on warm slippers and started a tour of the place that would become my home. I had hunkered down in the large bedroom at the back of the house.

As I entered the Main Room, I saw that Willow must have been here quietly checking on me. The cabin was warm and there were coals in the fireplace. Obviously, someone had restored the fire as it, the wood cookstove, and sunshine were the only source of heat this time of year.

A fresh loaf of homemade bread was on the cabinet by the stove along with some butter, nut butter and jam. All from 'scratch' not store bought. I realized I probably will learn a lot from this wonderful New Friend I met in the middle of a night. I touch the bread and find it has been here for a few hours, as it is cool – BUT FRESH.

As I ascended the stairs, I saw that both my bedroom suite and Sara's had come out here. They were in 2 of the upstairs bedrooms. Sara's at the back, and mine at the front where the door opened to the deck above the carport. These rooms had never had furniture as far as I could remember. We simply put out air mattresses and sleeping bags on the floor the few times we came out here.

Later, I found out that Willow had Joey and a couple of his buddies put the beds together and place the furniture. She had used 'the Directions' of her culture once she knew my birthdate. Where she got it from, I do not know.

Ah! But then I remember – she probably asked Grandad when he talked to her on the phone during his planning since the stuff would already be in the Cabin.

I decide that Peter and I shall have our bedrooms up here. Where Sara's furniture is, it is a large room. I still have room for a crib in the room.

It runs across the end of the house above the main floor bedroom. The front bedrooms are smaller in comparison. I will use one as a sleeping room, and the other as an office. Yes, both have doors to the deck and a view of the cove beyond.

Chapter 13

It took Peter and Naomi longer than expected to regain energy and be up to travels, or so it seemed. Altitude does have a bearing too. No matter.

It gave me, Jamie, and Tiny Peter time to get things unpacked and in place. We would make it a Festive Feel; after all, we would be celebrating my 21st Birthday – celebrating 'Jamie Gillette Parker's Official Introduction to her World.' It would be amazing to include Dr. Ben, the Daddy who named me. Too soon I suppose. Be patient please!

There were several legal pieces of mail when I got to the cabin and awakened enough to look after what was required. Henri and Marabella had not left me as stranded as I could have been.

It had never occurred to me that I might be financially strapped here in the cabin. Apparently, the death of my dear sister gave them funding for Peter and me.

Yet, I was surprised to find out that I was now the 'Owner' of this property and would require the income to look after it.

BUT first I must address the papers that _required me to change my name_. This had become a simple requirement for me. Little would I have guessed that I would soon be *"The DAUGHTER OF MY SIRE"* in more ways than one.

I became even more a part of Ben and his naming of me. From what I gathered; I Was A Love Child. Ben and Marabella were in love – Ben never once gave it a thought that he would not be the father of whatever the result might be. (Over the years, I have come to know that Ben never married because he was still very much in love with Marabella.)

What could I say, Dear Tiny Peter! Even in this we are loved, weird as it may seem.

Everyday, I either texted or talked to my Loved ones at their Rooms in Victoria. They knew the proceedings and the legalities I was faced with. Grandad was happy for me. I learned that this property was a Gift to Henri and Marabella from the Bokamosa Estate. Yes, happy twist after happy twist – but then that is how LOVE is braided!

Something seemed to keep delaying their getting in that Uber and coming to the Cabin, not that I minded as it gave me the extra time to get everything exactly right!

Thankful for the Bank Account started, and the Gift Card from Grandad when we got to Victoria: I could buy beds for the Guest Room downstairs. I also rigged up a kind of curtain wall to split the room in half. Grandad and Naomi could be close to each other, but not in the same bed. I understood that was important to their integrity.

I also bought a few zero recliners and a small table for the Great Room that included sitting area, dining and kitchen.

I would love to have painted the whole place and given it a fresh look before they got here. It was enough to get to know how to cook on a wood stove, go get water from the spring and all the other things involved in taking possession of Life and Living Full On.

Willow was a very patient teacher and interesting lady to get to know. She is a respected Life Coach and Author. She too, practices 'A Course in Miracles' and knows Dr David Hawkins work. We have that in common.

The ~~'Lonely'~~ and ~~'Isolated'~~ labels have been burned! There is nothing Lonely or Isolated about this place or the way of Life. In 1 week, I have settled in and have excellent teachers – yes, the whispering Willow just outside the window that tells me things I already know – it spreads curious shadows in the moonlight too. And then there are the Chickadees that constantly twitter in the trees or call Peetteri! Peetteri! Peetteri!

"Can you see Tiny Peter how much fun life is going to be in this place?"

When the whole horror of events cascaded down upon me the end of November, the death of my sister Sara the very day that Peter was conceived without my consent etc. I could not imagine the Fortunate Circumstances I was being led into.

"We are not ripped from Loved Ones Dear Peter; we are being given so much more!"

My excitement for Grandad and Naomi's arrival is reaching over the top. They are planning to arrive before dark on the 16th. Settle them in, and then by late afternoon on the 17th The Feast is Spread!

And Peter Dear little one, your Mom is not a scared and traumatize Petra anymore. She is becoming a Woman of Wisdom in the New Model as, Jamie Gillette Parker.

Yes, a part of American History. How could we have ever guessed!

"Who shall we invite Dear Peter?"
"Who do we even know?"

Well, we have Grandad and Naomi. We shall give them the Main Floor bedroom with the Porta Potti Willow fixed up. This will be rather primitive to what they are used to. I will buy extra buckets when we make our trip to town before they get here. I shall have lots of water in house, so I do not have to fetch it.

How much water per person? Now that is a huge question. I have never given water quantity a thought before now. I shall also get Solar lights to put in all the windows. I wonder if that would help to light the rooms at night?

Willow and Joey – ah I shall ask Joey to invite his Friends that helped him assemble the furniture here.

If we require more sleeping rooms, I will make up Sara's bed in your room Dear Peter. I wonder who might sleep there? Shall we imagine that Marabella would come?

Shall we imagine Dr. Ben would come?

My but we would have a Grand Housewarming!

This 'back to the basics lifestyle' is interesting. I never thought of us not having Power and Water in this Cabin. A couple of things I shall have to investigate before you are born. Washing diapers by hand does not appeal to me; but neither does paper/disposable diapering appeal to me.

Another question for Willow – how did she do it? Probably 'Moss Bag'. We both have a good laugh at this. I feel Peter move in my belly – signs of a living soul.

Willow has come to help me put the final touches on everything. We are non-alcoholic – all of us. She brought a gallon of her Fermented Tea called Kombucha – that is what Grandmother Karol served as well.

The Arrival! I hear the vehicle coming up the drive. It is rather steep, and I am glad for my Jeep 4-wheel drive. I hope the Uber driver has 4-wheel drive, especially since it snowed last night. There is no keeping me inside with company coming. Willow is right behind me out the door. They made it!

But there are FOUR?

It does not take long before we discover Grandad has another Surprise up his sleeve. No wonder it took extra time to '*Rest Up*'!

Naomi and then Grandad gives me a big hug. Grandad says "Well, I trust you will not mind, but I invited my Doctor to meet me in Victoria and join us for this week in the mountains." Silly! I knew perfectly well who 'his doctor was'.

At this point the Doctor steps around the vehicle to approach me. Grandad holds his hands toward the Doctor and says, "Dr. Benjamin Parker please meet my beloved granddaughter Jamie Gillette Parker" as he turns his hands toward me.

And what am I to do? Am I to go hug him? Am I to wait to see if he will hug me? What is expected of me in this moment?

It is not difficult to figure out – Dr. Ben brings something long out from behind him and walks toward me. With the long object held with both hands, he falls to his knees on the skiff of snow, bends his head in a bow and as he raises his head, he raises the object and says:

"I am offering you, Dear Jamie, The Peace Pipe, a symbol of the Circle of Kinship.

Know the Power of humility amongst the family of creation; understand your connection to all things living as well as to the Great Spirit who Creates from the LOVE that is everlasting.

Take the Pipe to offer a blessing, a prayer in respect and preservation of the diversity of Sacred Life. Daily Live from your Harmony with the Sacred Circle of Kinship."

He raised the pipe and himself. I put out both hands and take the pipe. It is beautifully carved and engraved. The natural knots and twists of the diamond willow wood gives it a uniqueness all its own. Though he used the words Peace Pipe, it is a Walking Stick he has carved himself.

Yes, I have a mantel over the fireplace – it will hang above to bring Peace & Love; and it will walk with Peter and I through the years.

We hug for a long time – 21 lost years.

Oh, how I wish my mother were here for this moment too!

I get Naomi to snap a photo of Ben and I holding the Peace Pipe.

I text it to my mother hoping she still has the same cell number.

Come what may.

AND THEN perhaps the Biggest Surprise ever. Willow and Ben know each other. They are relative though Ben is much younger than Willow. He is her cousin's child. Over the years when families gather, and the harvest is in, it is a time of sharing and looking after the needs of everyone, not just your own.

I learned that day that Willow was also a Lakota of the Sioux. Even more reason for us to all be together for the next days Celebration – my 21st Birthday.

I went to bed Thankful, like I had never been before for the Kinship of Creation. Thankful for who was gathered with me and maybe a little thankful for who was not.

There were none among us that were competitive or jealous of another. Or with the kind of low self esteem like Henri or Mara that gathered a lot of attention to the self instead of to the Good of the Whole.

"Peter you are entering an amazing relationship with Generous People Who LOVE."

Chapter 14

Before Grandad and Naomi left the Island, I drove them to see Henri and Marabella. Grandad had contacted them ahead of time. He was told that he would be welcome, but Henri wanted nothing to do with seeing Naomi or myself. Marabella would be at work. It would likely be best if they met at Starbucks Chapters. That way, Grandad could go with him to Starbucks and Naomi and I could roam around the Book Store.

Considerate of him! At least he remembered my Love of Books.

And that is how it went. I am sure Grandad had his portion of the Estate to gift him. However, in the public situation, and the way Henri treated him – as if to say, *'why are you interfering with my life?'* Grandad decided the Gift could wait for a future date. The visit ended in 20 minutes, and Grandad came in search of us ladies.

I saw Henri exit by the side door so that he would not have to face us in anyway. I felt for that man trapped in the Pharmaceutical Coma to cover his guilt and unforgiveness. Oh, how I wished that he could learn Ho'oponopono or use the Mirror Technique I learned long ago, as a Teen, actually from a Louise Hay Interview on YouTube.

Grandad arrange for a night in a Hotel before their plane left early in the morning the end of January for some time in Rochester with Dr. Ben.

Surprising to me, but he also arranged 2 extra nights for me to stay and do some shopping – all with a very sizable VISA Gift Card. And I knew with great certainty that this was not a Gift to Buy my Appreciation or to pay for any guilt he felt in not having enough time for me. I had no question that this was a Gift of True LOVE.

I prayed that God would keep Grandad and Naomi in good health for at least another 10 years. I wanted to see them again and hoped they would be alive and well enough to come visit The Cabin for Peter's birthday some year.

I was glad for the time at the Hotel. It gave my tears time to fall before the long drive back to the cabin. Yet, I did not wish to be messed up emotionally for long. So mid morning, I showered and went out for lunch and shopping.

Oh, how I wished that Petri was in town and I could visit him over that lunch, or even for Dinner that evening.

Instead, after buying up some bargains and looking into Solar Panels etc. I returned to the hotel and ordered-in while I read the Books on pregnancy I had chosen while Henri and Grandad had their visit the day before.

Yes, it hurt my heart to not see my Mother and share all the Joy of the past few weeks. The joy of meeting her family and falling in love with them.

I knew it was time to disconnect. They had already pulled the plug – literally. It was time for me at 21 to become TRANS PARENT. To let go of attachments to the past and listen more intently to my own InnerNet for guidance.

NOWING!

Ho'oponopono the past and the people of the past to LOVE NOW; to experience the Curiosity of the NOW; embracing the emotional and environmental harmony like never before.

Chapter 15

Winter passed into Spring. My belly is obvious and a little awkward to bend and do exercises. I have a few solar panels on the roof now that provides me with enough power for the computer and internet.

I plan to stay off grid if I can. I am growing fond of the daily routines required for just providing what I need each day. By next spring, I may even get chickens.

A Bath is a Luxury indeed! And to think Dear Willow provided it for me on my arrival. Dear Soul, that she is. I am coming to love her more and more. She is about Naomi's age. I have learned that she was raised for the most part in a foster home until she was 16 and thought she knew more than she did.

She found out that she did not fit in to her native culture anymore than she fit into a Caucasian Culture. Fortunately, she has of great respect for the Great Spirit and began studies in Sociology and many of the areas of my own interest – though she has more than 3 times my age - 100 times the wisdom.

Joey helped me work up a garden patch for basic veggies and salad greens for the summer. In the spring Willow showed me the leaves of weeds in my yard that I could eat.

I am learning to fish in the cove. Maybe half my meat is fish now. Fresh pan fried is simply the best. I have also roasted them over an open fire down by the beach. Yummy!

My little Peter will have lots of learning experiences ahead of him come August. No, I have not been to a doctor as such. I did get Ben to check things out before he left to be sure all was in order. He advised me that Willow knew all the care I would require. She is a Midwife among other things. So, I am trusting. Once I got over the initial morning sickness, I have had no complaints. Willow says Keep Active and I will be fine.

As Spring passed into Summer, eating from the garden is simply wonderful compared to the produce of the store. We do have a local market every Friday afternoon. I like to go to see what there is to grow that I do not grow now. Yes, WEEDS! Joey assures me that as a garden has a couple of years I will not have as many. Willow tells me to eat them and that will get rid of them too.

I have not heard from my parents. I have not tried to keep in touch either. I have Family Larger than I ever expected.

I have a text from Naomi or Grandad and Ben almost every day. We text back and forth for a few moments.

It seems that Mara is enjoying her new place, but lonely. She does not have as much to gossip with her ladies' clubs. She is not as interesting, so they do not invite her as often. She has chosen a Landscape Company that does several yards in her area. So contrary to what she wanted for the Estate.

Peter and Maria often text as well.

From what I gathered from different communications with relatives in Africa is that Henri did go to Leipzig. Not in January, but for the next Session in March. Marabella told Karol that he spent a lot of time packing the motorhome, cleaning out the garage and figuring out a way to haul his small car behind it. Why he needed all that to go to a Health Center, she did not know at the time. However, it was evident later that he had not thought of returning. He took what was his and a sizable chunk of the Bank Account the day he left for Saskatchewan.

Marabella followed her heart and went for 3 weeks in Sedona Arizona. She booked in at a Wellness Spa and fully enjoyed her time to herself. According to Karol, she came back to work a new woman more engaged with her heart and the Wellness of her body and mind. She had told her mother that she went through a lot of Emotional Treatment at the Spa as well.

She could understand Henri better, and herself even more. She said she dealt with her attitude toward her father. She looked at her attitudes as a Workaholic to cover what she did not want to see emotionally. And yes, she dealt with the remorse she felt toward the way her daughters turned out.

When she got home there was a Divorce Order from Henri. It came from the Lawyer. At that point, she knew it was over and his intentions.

Fortunately, Marabella was still working and still had the house in her name. Whether he went alone or not, she did not know, and she really did not care – it was as if she had lost 195 pounds of dead weight. It was a relief that she could start a New. Twenty-two years of nightmares were enough with a Narcissistic Partner.

It did mean that she had to sell the house and move into a rental to pay off the debts he left her with. However, I heard via the grapevine that Grandad gave the Gift he was going to give to Henri to Marabella. A responsible choice as far as I can see.

Of course, I am getting ahead of myself as these communications have come over a few years now.

I know Grandma Karol was softening her toward my situation as well. Softening her toward all she was missing of her Grandson. I had sent her a birth announcement and his 1st year of photos. However, when his envelop was returned because of no forwarding address, I stopped sending. I really did not have any idea of where she was either. Her cell phone had obviously changed as well.

Yes, it took over five years to break the grip her attitudes claimed about me. In the end it was all very surprising as to how she made the switch and we have been the best of friends ever since.

As for Henri, she does not know where he is or even if he went to Leipzig in the end. I probably know more about his where abouts as I hear occasionally what Grandad has heard through Mara – tragic as it seems, apparently his motorhome was found at the end of a forestry road, beyond a tight curve – chard and mangled about a year after he left for Leipzig. The remains of 2 bodies were within. The identifier was that the car had come unhooked in the tumble and was not burned.

Every day is full of love and communication. Besides Studies of course.

Mid August is soon upon us. I am both excited and apprehensive – do I know enough? Have I done right what I have done during pregnancy? Am I making the right choice for my Baby in being a single parent instead of offering it for adoption to a two-parent home? I gave this a lot of thought and felt I was the Parent the child required. I have so much support in my community to assist both of us in growing.

I have chosen to have Peter as natural as I can with Willows Coaching. We have been doing the pre-birth exercises for a month now. Willow tells me that Ben will be out to visit on his vacation mid August. I wonder if he is planning it as 'a just in case'. Someone with Gynecological Training in case a back up is required. Willow sees no reason for it as she has been regularly doing examinations and monitoring position of Dear Peter.

I will deliver in a squat position. Also, he could be born a Water Baby if I want to venture out into the cove. It will all depend on the temperature of the day.

And so Gardening fills a lot of my day. In the early morning is my time to Study.

Chapter 16

It is a Gorgeous Day as only August can present. I receive a text from Karol that Dr. Karabo slipped away quietly this morning or evening, whatever the time over there. It is said that when a Soul leave the Earth, another is Born to take their place. I wonder "Will Peter decide to come today, the day that Papa Karabo left for regions beyond? Afterall, he was conceived the day that Sara left the earth plain."

Here on the Island the temperature is comfortably warm but not excruciatingly hot. To me the 3rd week in August is one we can depend upon to be a Perfect Weather Week to plan an outing of any kind and obviously Peter agrees.

Near the Spring is a large Water Willow. Joey and Willow helped me put up a Birthing Tipi. We have placed everything we need for Peter's arrival.

Besides many other things, Willow is teaching me Ways of the Universe – how we are connected to all things. Ben has also become an avid teacher of the ways of my Ancestors. He is a brilliant man and knows how to match the science with the traditions.

Willow knows a lot about Energy and does Energy Work. Let us see what I have learned so far that we are not taught in textbooks or school?

Everything is Vibrating Energy, even our thoughts – keep the Good Ones.

Things vibrate at different frequencies. The higher frequencies are higher and more positive. A frequency above a frequency is often the healer of a lower frequency.

If I do not like whatever happened in the past, change the energy around it to become what I would prefer – it is all a matter of Perception anyway.

There are only 4 reasons behind dis-ease:

1. Structural Alignment – if the Spine is miss aligned messages cannot travel the nerve system so well.
2. Malnutrition – I can be eating a lot, but if it just fills my tummy and does not feed the Brain or cells for growth, I am looking malnutrition in the face. What I put on my skin is also absorbed – Is it chemical from natural gases or is it a food source? I also learn that too much sugar is a drain on my brain and makes me tired – it will for tiny Peter too.
3. Emotions – yes, emotions are a huge one. Something that I do have control over. If I do not like the Perception I am looking through, change the *Energy in Motion* (the feelings) that I am perceiving it through. Sounds easy but we buy into a lot of negativity, especially if we are being bombarded by the negative news on radio and TV. Fortunately, I have chosen (all my life really) to limit that information. I never did see the value of being up to date with the negative side of humanity. I choose not to live in fear.
4. And now Willow says that a lot of folks have Environmental Allergies, especially those who live in populated and industrial environments or have not had a natural food supply. We are also getting a lot in our food – chemical toxicity through air

pollution and chemicals sprayed on food sources that were not here prior to the end of the Second World War.

Another reason for seeing my Cabin as the right place to raise my little Peter. I would not have believed I was to become such a Native Lover as I am 10 months ago.

I was so enjoying the African relatives and adventures that I was planning to stay there and put down roots again as Grandad had even supplied me with the property to do so.

Anyway, here I am and SO BLESSED!

Exactly 24 hours after his 100-year-old Great-Great Grand Father left for his eternal life, comforted by the harmonious songs of relatives close by his bed. Their singing from the end of December rings in my ears yet.

I am 21 years and 7 months older than my Peter. He arrived that very afternoon as the sun shone from the west through the Tipi door. However, I was not in the Tipi. Ben relaxed in a lawn chair not far away – The *Just in case* Doctor on Call! They had come when I was feeling the first pangs of more than a little movement of Peter swimming in amniotic fluids.

Willow and I were under the Water Willow. It was an old tree with large branches. She had placed a rubber sheet over a low limb that I could squat over so my legs did not get too weary in the process. But first she had me go into the Spring Flow and allow my body to relax as I deep breathe. The water is cool but not uncomfortably cold. I feel Peter low in the birthing canal. It is like the flowing water encourages him to flow out into the open air.

Perhaps there is nothing easy about Birthing. I count myself lucky. I am young. I am strong as I have been doing a lot of walking up and down to the Cove along with Gardening and the general of carrying water and wood. You name it.

Soon Peter punches through the water sack. When the flow stops, I carefully step over the rocks and position my Squat near the willow – nothing is going to stop him from showing his face to the world on this gorgeous day – August 17.

No, he was not wearing a mask – well not yet at least. I was hoping I could raise him **with love for Who He Is** rather than for who he believed others wanted him to be. And here he was! Willow's gentle hands on my belly encouraged his descent.

It helps to have someone near that knows what they are doing, knows what you are doing and knows what is safe for baby. It was not long in comparison to some. For 2 hours, Willow and Ben sang and whistled back and forth as Birds Sing in the forest. Their native songs relaxed and settled me into the process of easily opening the Birth Canal.

The pain stopped and I thought how Beautiful the music and the process of the passed few hours!

She cleared away what required clearing away as I heard his intake of air – fresh and pure near the spring that flowed to the cove below and the ocean beyond.

Both in the nakedness of our Being – Mother & Son. She had placed a dark haired, dark eyed bundle of flesh in my arms.

Pure Joy filled my being – yes, I had heard his birth cry but only for a few moments. In my arms, he was full of curiosity about his surroundings just as I was about him. So tiny and yet so observant of all that was around him. The sunlight between the willow leaves seemed to intrigue him. I followed his eyes as he observed the very slight breeze in the leaves.

I was told that babies do not see clearly for several weeks. If Peter was not seeing clearly, he certainly was seeing something.

I knew there was a pair of stray Cardinals had a nest in these willows. A song and communication began to take place above us – Love, Connection, and Protection.

A Jay called and flew into the tree just above us. Peetteri followed the Blue Jays flight. Obviously, he heard the voice – not a whisper.

An Oriel, flute trilled its song near by.

Aware of all these birds honoring Birth – New Life thrilled me. Even the Chickadees were all a flutter and twitter. We were all one Family of the Earth united in birth, in Harmony with the All-Creative Source of LOVE within us all.

Peace on/in Earth and Good Will to all Humanity – My Peter is a Living Soul.

I was not even aware of my nakedness in this simple harmony of oxytocin and the warmth of the afternoon. Though Peter was no longer inside we were still one with the Universe.

Willow draped a terry blanket about us to dry us off and encourage us to rest in the tipi. As we settled in, Peetteri decided it was supper time as well. He began to whimper and search for my nipple. Amazing that he learned so quickly exactly what he required.

Ben and Willow quietly left us to ourselves – and we slept.

Chapter 17

Time passes when you are having fun as they say. Did you ever wonder about 'they say' as in who are *they anyway*? I have wondered often.

I have been so thankful that I have Ben and Willow to share Peetteri with. When Family rejects you the Creator always gives you something even better. Well Peter is growing and learning so many things every year. We have chickens now and a couple of milking goats. They fascinate him. He is learning to milk and considers the animals 'his chores'.

I am still in contact with my South African relatives almost daily. Every August we can expect some of the African Family for Peter's Birthday. We look forward to their visits.

As for Henri and Marabella, we hear little. Peter is almost 5 this summer and they have not set eyes upon him. (yes, I did hear of Henri's possible death.) I sent photos until the mail was returned the 2nd year and I quit.

To be honest, other than being at the Airport in Victoria, I have seldom been back there since my return from Africa with Grandad and Naomi. I did drive Grandad and Naomi to see them after they were here for my 21st birthday. It was a very brief visit for them, and I was asked to remain in the vehicle. Nice Welcome back! Of course, I wonder if my Mom even knew. She was working and I do not believe Henri communicated the visit to her or with her.

Anyway, I have nothing to complain about. I have an excellent parent in Ben. We are Soulmates in the pattern of our thoughts.

And Willow too. Maybe I am more Native American than Dutch South African after all. I only wish I could share my excitement about all of life with my Mother as well. She has no idea of what she is missing. No, she has not consented to meet up with Ben either even though I know that Henri is no longer a burden to her; that he too had a life cut short.

I wonder if she still lives on the Island or did, she disappear too? Grandmother Karol will know.

About the time Peter was a year old I did drive around my old home and school just to show him my home, as if he could remember at such a young age. Anyway, maybe I was just a little lonely. I did see a big For Sale sign on our home property. I know they sold their business and mom is still working at the hospital.

Maybe I was a little lonely for companionship as well. I really hoped that in some way I could align with Petri. I have no idea where he is or what he is doing these days. Why we never kept track of each other is still a mystery to me. Maybe the course of things as my mother never kept track of Ben either.

Peetteri does look a lot like him. From Naomi's idea that I could choose whoever I wished and whatever situation I wished to be the conception of Peter, I chose Petri as his father and a camping trip before we both left for distant shores. Not something we did but a sweeter perception.

Of course, Peetteri would be 3 or 4 months overdue for that to be true. No matter, he does look enough like Petri for it to be so.

Will I ever meet him again? I am told that his mother passed into eternity a year after Sara. I wonder if Petri ever met his brother. 20 years is a generation difference in age. Think of Peetteri being 20 before I would have another child – Hilarious!

Today Ben is at Willow's and Little Peter is with them. He had a 'sleep over'. Whether he is entertaining them or them he, it might be interesting. I appreciate that Ben comes as often as he does. He is always here for Peter's birthdays. Mostly he lodges at Willow's, his cousin

I am on my way to the city to do some shopping for the Birthday Party on Saturday. His last birthday before School Years keeps him occupied. Dollarama and The Party Store along with groceries are my route. Yes, treats but not very many. We prefer health rather than overindulgence. Interesting how Peetteri does not even like sweets. He has always said "ucky" to them.

The cake will be Carrot Cake made with fresh carrots from our garden, and half the honey instead of sugar. Cream cheese icing will balance the proteins too. Yes, we will include Peter Rabbit along with the carrots on top.

This year Grandad and Naomi are coming. What a surprise. An even bigger surprise is that Karol Karabo is coming this year. Great Grandma died in the spring, so she is free of their care.

They fly up from Victoria on the same plane. It is possible that Naomi and Karol will recognize each other from our Cape Town holiday before Peter was born. We will pick them all up at the same time. Peetteri knows they are coming. He is old enough to be quite excited about meeting the Plane.

Missing is my Mom. My heart twinges and tears try to force their way to the surface. I know she is the one choosing and losing. I know my tears will not help and yet LOVE so desires to have her nearby.

Another Gorgeous Day in August. 5 years is a flash of time and growth.

We are gathered on a Saturday afternoon to Celebrate Peter Benjamin Parker. Three boys from the swim team, 3 Great Grandparents – AND I MEAN GREAT, and Papa along with the Hostess yours truly; what could make for a better party? Well, if my Mother, Marabella, were here too.

The boys have gone to play in the spring. Peter and I have worked over the years to make a Basin at the bottom of the falls before it takes a slower route down the hill to the beach. The Basin allows for the water to warm and make it nice to soak up the sun in. Perhaps it is our bathing tub for a good part of the year.

We are all sitting under the Water Willow nearby. There is great conversation going on from 2 continents a world apart and even half a country apart in South Africa. I am enjoying serving and bring a wagon full of goodies to the picnic table.

Chapter 18

Between Willow and I we seem to invest a lot of time in travel to Coach our Frolics and Book Tours. So, time certainly does fly! A good education for Peter as he is in the company of highly influential folks. We all assist each other in our Tours and Classes, which is a plus, and we have Joey back home to look after things while we are away.

It is another Gorgeous Day in August. 7 years is a flash of time and growth. I wonder who has grown most Peter or me?

We are gathered again to Celebrate Peter Benjamin Parker. Yes, The Man of the House! His three buddies are with us again. As I said before the third week in August is always fine weather.

Karol, Grandad, and Naomi are keeping every 2 years free to come as long as they are able. We honor their presence. Papa Ben comes for most of the summer now.

And as the Hostess 'Yours Truly'; what could make for a better party? Well, if my Mother, Marabella, were here too. I think I recite the above every August 17. Not always have the Greats been with us, but Papa Ben has not missed.

The boys have gone to play in the spring while the adults visit and eat of course.

We are all sitting under the Willow nearby. I am enjoying serving and bring a wagon full of goodies to the picnic table.

Yes, we have the Tradition of sharing the Kombucha – mine is usually Raspberry, whereas Willow prefers the Peach. Karol is here this year, and she creates a variety of flavors. She is here for the summer. We are both hoping that Marabella will consider inviting Karol to wherever she is living after the party.

The building Project has been delayed as Jack was called out of the country on an Urgent Family Matter. So perhaps this is the last birthday celebration before the Mess starts for however long it takes.

It is about 4:30 p.m. Voices stop and splashing stops. Even the Birds seem to stop and listen. It is seldom that we would hear the roar of a motorbike out here. But we do!

All eyes turn toward the trail leading up to my Cabin as the noise seems to get nearer and nearer. We see not 1 but 2 Red Harley Davidsons. I am thankful for the Male Power with me today. Might be scary if Peter and I were by ourselves. Who knows what could happen, or who it would even be? I do not know anyone who has a Big Bike or even a desire to ride such a noisy vehicle.

We all just sit in silence staring and waiting.

They park by the Jeep. (yes, I still have my trusty old orange Jeep that grandad Peter gave me for my 16th birthday.)

They see us, and we see them. It is a tall slim man and a woman about the size of Karol. Even the boys are not off and running to seize the opportunity to investigate the Harleys.

The couple take off their biking gear and start to walk our way. They are smiling and bearing gifts, which surprises me, but not Peter. Noticing the Gift bags, he heads out running toward them just as a curious child does. His friends in hot pursuit.

The man takes the packages, and the woman scoops up the seven-year-old in a very tight embrace. My Peter is still small of stature.

Karol is the first to recognize her LOVE might be working in one of the Bikers and starts toward them with open arms. And then I know it must be my Mother, Marabella.

Oh, Joyous Day!

Karol and Marabella embrace for a long time with tears. Soon they reach the group and Marabella introduces us to Paul Price. Almost before she finishes saying his name, she has me in her arms with a hug so strong and long, that it must be making up for over 7 years of absence. We are both sobbing tears of Joy. They have a different chemical make up than tears of sadness. I can even taste the difference.

But I do wonder how long the relationship will last.

Stop! Why does my human thought always have to surface to spoil what is otherwise a perfect day?

Marabella and I began again. She felt as rejected by me as I by her. She did not know Henri had a visit with Peter Sr. She did not receive either the birth photos or the Birthday cards I had sent.

When Henri left, he had mail forwarded to who knows where, except for the bills belonging to the home and lawyer. Anything the included Henri or Mr. was forwarded – maybe to weir-wolf land? Of course, I had sent them Mr. & Mrs. – common etiquette.

She had let her cell phone go for a new one with the letting go of the Henri era, as he continued to harass her with TEXTS. Even though I had texted her, she could not believe I meant my love after the initial rejections Henri orchestrated.

I felt so sorry for my Dear Mother. So many hurts and hurtles for her to get through, very similar to my own childhood. The difference – I had been collecting Tools; she chose to stuff and bury not recognizing that they only smolder under the surface and control us in more ways than we wish to acknowledge.

I chose to Ho'oponopono. I had a lot of relative support. She seemed to think she had none, as she kept her hurts and did not accept the family of love. Instead, she became a workaholic – bury what is a controller in the needs of others rather than look at our own. That way we think we do not have to face ourselves. Her yearly trips to Sedona, and the weekly sessions she had from a Coach there, has brought her a long way in her healing.
Secretly, I believe the death of Henri and her new found appreciation from Paul has an enormous benefit as well.

She is learning with Paul, what Petri taught me so many years ago – That I Mattered.

Chapter 19

Peter is in his Tower above my Studio where he has his Telescope that Papa Parker gave him for his 7th birthday. Hopefully, he is studying. His room is not quite as large as mine.

One of the requests I had for Jack was the possibility of the roof to this Tower being on a Swivel somehow that we could swing it off to the open sky. I wanted Peter to have full access to the night sky if he wishes to look at the star constellations.

Jack said it was possible though he would have to do some research as the best way to do it and with what materials so that it would be light enough to be movable, insulated against the cold and sealable.

Ta Dah! And he had it built just that way. I believe Jack is in Love with Peter as much as I am. He teaches us a lot about Living Curious and then Observing the results to see what an even better plan next time would be. I love the Child Curious Way. I am learning to live that as well. I am teaching my Tribe the same.

My mind is flashing back to Cape Town a distant memory now. So much to enjoy and remember of the excitement that New Years Eve – So many names and faces on my cell phone camera to reminisce for years to come.

Time is passing quickly. I feel moved to take Peter to meet relatives as an eleventh birthday gift. I have a couple of years to plan.

The project is pretty much finished now, and we can relax into the enjoyment thereof and the employment of having folks come to us for a quiet writing experience or when Willow and I decide to do a 3 Day Frolic.

I love the idea that we can do it from the new cabins and the Longhouse. I enjoyed working with Willow in the planning. Ben's suggestions were greatly appreciated as well. An All-Nations Project coming together in one place.

Of course, I could not have done all the Upgrades we did if it were not for Grandad Peter's financial help. It turns out that the Estate House and acreage close around it was to be Sara and my inheritance. Grandad could see that it was not the best plan, so the money it sold for, became my inheritance to build here.

Yes, my books bring in money; my coaching brings in money; and I am still getting the money from Sara's Insurance. But still the project is huge. Now that it is all but finished the advertising goes out to Book Retreats and Frolics of all sorts. Willow and I have figured out a good plan for charging folks to use the facility etc.

No more packing up the things we need to travel distances to share all the wisdom Willow, and all the care and techniques she taught me to share as well.

Grandad Peter's financial support was a surprise to me. What would have been mine in South Africa, when sold, was invested, along with Sara's portion, to eventually be invested in the Cove property. You might say I was doubly blessed, though I lost a sibling.

When I started talking remodel and expand, Grandad confided to me what was waiting to be invested in the project. But first, Peter Sr. Style, he asked what the **<u>Dream Project</u>** would be? Beyond the initial idea of renovating and upgrading the Cabin, what was my Dream? Just as he had asked what my Dream Bokamosa Diamond something would look like.

Jack Williams has claimed the 1st Event. He is bringing his Staff up here for their Year End Event in a couple of weeks. I like Jack and he seems to be a little interested in me. He and Peter get on very well. Like Father and Son which brings my heart Joy. There is a resemblance between the gardener and Jack. They are both from East Indian heritage; maybe that is all.

Sometime when Jack comes up for a few days to relax and we can get to know each other from a personal relationship instead of a work/project relationship I have a load of questions to ask.

Yes, the first has already been answered – he is not married and does not have attachments for which I am glad. He is so much like Petri was in high school. Sometimes I catch myself wanting to call him Petri too.

Chapter 20

Messages from the InnerNet!

Think how whole we are from whom the Voice of Creation calls lovingly to our neighbor – They have come. We awaken in them the whisper, and it is The Great Spirit that answers our call!

We think how whole they are when in them sleeps our own LOVE, with our freedoms joined with the Great Spirit!

When we wish others condemned, remember the Great Spirit is Eternal LOVE, and in them too. We will never know The Creator in ourselves if we attack The Chosen Tipi in another and believe we battle with its Brave. Respect others graciously. We look with loving eyes on them who carry LOVE within themselves, we behold the glory and rejoice that The Great Sky is not separate from us when LOVE dwells in us.

We are simply asked to trust those who carry LOVE with us, forgiven of all errors just as we forgive others of the errors, we believed were against us.

Keep some tiny hurt we cherish, and the shadow between us obscures Eternal LOVE and the memory of Creation. Why would we trade LOVE and the memory of Creation for an ancient wound?

We stand on Wholly ground because of all who stand with us who have blessed it with their LOVE, their innocence, their Joy, and their peace. Upon this Space called Earth the radiant blooms shine the LOVE in the full Son's Light. What once we thought a place of death is now the Tipi of Light because we are At ONE with the eternal Great Spirit of LOVE.

The Great Spirit lifts wholeness to take its place in the Eternal Circle that always was and always will be, even if we fail to see what LOVE & LIGHT would have us see.

The Miracle - what resentment brought is undone to stand in LOVE, as The Arms of what is beyond Sky enfolds us to join with all who LOVE. At this moment, the illusion of separateness vanishes to nothingness – We have let the LOVE our neighbor holds come within. The LOVE! The Knowing! The LIGHT! The Eternal Circle of Kinship every flowing!

What resentment claimed, is now given up to LOVING. Freedom lights up every living thing and lifts us into The Eternal Circle where the light grows brighter as each soul comes home. The incomplete now complete again as The Great Spirit's Joy increases with the restoration of what was always its own.

Let go of all illusions and battle terminology to embrace and empower the LOVE that we always were. The battle-scarred earth is cleansed, the garments of insanity dropped to atone as ONE with the Whole, Blessed in Eternal LOVE.

And Eternal Gratitude Shines again within this Gift of The Present.

Vulnerable!

Transparent!

LOVE is come to gather in Its Own; unlocked what was held apart from LIGHT: no longer fearing our vulnerability we recognize that LOVE has never been against us but Blessing us in every experience.

Transparent as a Small Child, the LIGHT NOW floods any darkness, releasing any fear to gather the Essence of Eternal LOVE in every Soul. The holiest place on Earth is where a long-ago hurt becomes a Present LOVE.

"We are sorry.
"Please forgive us.
"Thank You.
"We LOVE You."

This Is the song of Our Soul until it is so transparent that the LOVE LIGHT has totally obscured any trace of the memory. Through this LOVE of Souls, we let go of any lingering resentment toward anyone we held responsible for *the inappropriate touching and/or invasion of our innocence and virginity.*

Only then can we wholly enter Eternal LOVE again to complete the journey we agreed to take through Time and Space, to return to the Ancient LOVE that always was and always will be.

We again Enter the Living Tipi where a cot for us is set up. There is no place more Whole in all the cycle of Eternal LOVE. What indignation has released to LOVE becomes the Brightest Light, radiating to penetrate the darkness of whatever may be left behind.

Those who still in fear of LIGHT may seek to hide beneath the rocks – yet how could anyone wish to resist the LOVE that LIGHTS the Soul with such Grace and Blessing?

Should they choose to live their greed, their lust in sorcery *(charmers with drugs)* still, we are Free of any guilt the *'nervous system remembers'.*

We continue to LOVE the Soul of all humanity without placing any human judgement upon them.

We climbed beyond the experiences we once thought *'tragic'* to forgive and Let Go of anything that may hinder our LOVE'S Completeness; wrapped in the Wings of the Great Spirit.

Chapter 21

Discovery – At last a little Romance that I have not had since Graduation and Petri was home as my Escort.

The Eight Octagon Cabins encircle the Wash House. It is spectacular. Something that has been my Dream since a Teen and studying ACIM and Feng Shui. People have a series of Good Directions and not so good directions. Rent the Cabin with the furnishings in your Best directions.

Willow and I can always change the arrangement to Honor their Best Wellness Direction for sleeping. The Desk would be on the angle that Honored their Best Work/Income direction etc. We now have it! It is time to name this place.

My Desire was to have a Coaching Compound that had 8 Sleeping Cabins around the Washhouse; each with a board walk to the Washhouse. A kind of Octagon Garden Courtyard within the larger Octagon.

The Cabin has worked up to now; but both Willow and I will be conducting Frolic/Retreats from here as well as Coaches who choose to rent the facility.

The Cabin has been updated with beauty in every room. This is Peter and my Home! Yes, we both have a Sanctuary in the Tower that rises high on the west side overlooking the Cove. The Carport and Deck above are now beneath my gorgeous Space with windows on three sides to take in the beauty of a space in nature beyond words.

Peters stairs continues up from mine to the top of the Tower. His ceiling can be pivoted to the side to reveal the night sky.

With the help of our Hero's, Willow, Ben and Jack, we have decided upon "**Discover Dreams above Curiosity Cove**". A little more Romantic than 'the Cabin' because it is more than a Cabin now.

It is a Dream Come True!

It is spring and we have hosted a few Groups already. Jack Williams Inc. was our first as their Year End Retreat.

Willow and I have hosted:

Mid January - 'Feature Your Future Now (FYFN). It is one we expect to honor every January.

In February, A Quilters Group rented.

And the two of us had a The Heart of Couple Frolic over the Valentine weekend.

March brought us a Scrap Booking Group.

We are happy with the results of this amazing project.

Thanks to so many folks who LOVE in my life, I am again in Awe of how the Creator gives and gives and gives some more when we align with All Creation.

Over the past months into a year, Jack has been questioning me more and more about my work with ACIM and Feng Shui. He asked at one point for his 'Directions'. I took note that his birthday is what I remember Petri's birthday was; maybe similar energy being the same birth date.

I noticed that the Octagon with windows to the falls and cove was the first to be finished after the washhouse completion. Jack claims it as his own. Interesting!

This weekend, he has asked to rent that Octagon for 'a week to recharge', he says. Not that I would even think of 'renting' to him. He has become too good a friend to Peter to charge him. Anyway, the thought of having him around without being full of work and leadership intrigues me.

As the weekend passed, I could not have imagined the sense of Family I felt, Peter felt, and I believe Jack also felt. How I missed the companionship of a Male that loved what I loved and could converse easily. I did not have that sense of Family after leaving Peter in Africa, and Petri before that. And here we were.

– Family within the Family of all things Living!

This is LOVE that is beyond human love.

Sunday Willow and Joey came for lunch. We have a Picnic Shelter under the Willow at the Spring. Yes, the Tipi is still standing as well. Of course, we maintain it for special occasions. It is the Birthplace of Peter the third.

About mid afternoon, Willow suggested that she required Peter to help her with a project and suggested that he bring along his nap sack for the night. Yes, I caught the wink between Jack and Willow so no protest on my part. Yes, I wanted time to converse with Jack by ourselves as well.

I wanted to discover his background, which I knew little of up to this point. It seemed he knew more about me than I wished anyone to know; but then again Jack and both Ben and Grandad seemed to relate very well to each other last summer at Peter's birthday. Maybe that was a male thing.

"And so, it is!" as Grandad often said.

This was the first time Jack and I had gone alone to the sandbar in the Cove. Yes, hand in hand! No one had held my hand since Grad Weekend. This felt so right; and yet my insides questioned motives. Why did human reasoning have to butt into something so spectacular and so right in the moment?

The sandbar was not enough. After all, we knew it as Curiosity Cove by now. As playful children we walked hand in hand into the water. Jack asked if I could swim?

"Can you?" I asked.

Soon we stepped as far as the drop off and it was swim or sink. We swam the short distance to the opposite bank and pulled ourselves out by grabbing a low willow branch. And there we sat with only our feet in the water and our wet clothes clinging to our bodies. His arm around my shoulders and the water running off intermingled from us both.

I wondered if our thoughts were along the same thread – Our lives intermingled just as the water between us was flowing back to the ocean together? We sat for a long time without words.

Finally, I broke the silence with the question that had surfaced so many times in the past months – "Jack tell me about your history? Where did you grow up and go to school?"

I believe I was expecting him to tell me he was born in India or the middle east somewhere.

"I knew you needed to know. One of the reasons I stayed on this weekend. Willow and I arranged for Peter to have this time with them, so I could have this time with you Dear Jamie" as he squeezed me in even closer. "I know that this may not be an easy conversation."

"Jamie, this isn't the first time we have been this close. Maybe not this wet" he teased.

"This is not the first time we have spent a weekend together. This isn't the first time we have communicated on more than a business level."

I wondered if he was talking in a past lives.

Jack suggested we swim back across the stream and go get dried off before we get deep into this communication. When we struck sand under our feet and could stand, Jack enveloped me in a huge hug.

"I have been waiting way too long to devour your Goodness and Beauty dear Jamie. I sense your concerns; so, do not let me rush you. We have a lot to catch up on. It is an emotional time for me too. Yes, I know 'I am a man' and '*I can handle anything*'. I know those lines way too well. But maybe I can't without assistance from someone who knows."

Hand in hand we ascended the steps up to the Cabin level in silence. We both went our own way to dry off and get some fresh clothes on. And met back on the Balcony over the carport. Jack's team had built an impressive exterior staircase up to it.

I reflect that 10 years has made an impressive difference in this property. Who would have thought a childhood dream could become this amazingly magnificent and yet blend into the woodland surrounding!

Jack carried a familiar box, though worn from travels. He set it on the floor beside the settee.

Once settled in, he continued "Do you remember Crescent Heights High?"

"Indeed, I do sir!"

"Do you remember the Library?"

"Another match – I do."

He reached into the box and pulled out a well-read Blue Book – "Do you remember this, the day we sat across the table with the Same Book?"

"We began to study the book ACIM together until our lives took a turn in opposite directions. I have often chastised myself as to why I never followed up with you by keeping in touch in some way. I guess I unconsciously thought you would always be there when I came home. Well, today I am in touch literally" as he turned to face me, our eyes looking deep into the other's soul. The intensity of Grad Weekend Remembered.

He need not tell me, but he did. "Petra, I am Petri." Even so, a deep sigh escaped my soul. So long I had waited his return and here we were. Now I recognized why we felt so familiar over the past couple of years working together.

Jack brought the box forward and began to take out the contents. "Jamie do you recognize this?"

Of course, I did. As we both held the Dream Catcher in front of us. My fingers traced the lines of the old painting. As I said before, "I could not replicate or even tell you the techniques used – it Just *is*!" and we sat it aside.

"Jack, what prompted you to change your name?"

"Jamie, I ask you the same, but first I will answer your question. My mother died in my 3rd year of Architecture College. As both my parents worked in a Laboratory, I can see why they named me what they did and being an east Indian name. I saw no reason to be 'A Petri Dish' as an Architect. I have a brother 20 years older, whom I had never met at that time. When my Mother died, I tried to contact him to share in the estate. He was nowhere to be found. I assumed he must have died without us knowing."

"So, we both have a sibling who died. Accept I knew my sister more deeply than you knew your brother."

"Yes, Jamie but I have since found out my brother is not dead. I'll add to that later."

"Back to Jack Williams – the name popped into my head and I thought 'why not' it is a good British name – if you remember, I was Studying in England. And no, I chose not to have a middle name."

"And now Jamie it is your turn?"

"When I was in Africa, I discovered that Henri was not my birthright. I discovered many deceptions and hidden identities in my history. More so in his history. He was not even Grandad's son, but his half brother. Grandad Peter's father was not a man of integrity as Grandad is. You have met Naomi which is Grandad's 'Forever Friend', but you have not met Mara."

"Mara was a street girl whose mother came to work for the Bokamosa Estate when Grandad Peter's mother was not well. When she was 14 David Bokamosa took her to bed. Grandad came home from Duty and found himself already married to Mara. 6 months later, the first child David was born."

"Two years later when Peter was away training at another mine for 4 months, Henri was conceived by the same man. David Sr. died when Henri was 5. Of course, they were both supposed to be Peter's boys, which I am proud of Grandad for doing the fatherly part in the best way he could with a contentious wife. Probably contentious because of her own ill behavior; though I wonder how much trauma that woman took in early life too."

"After his father, David died, Peter did conceive a daughter with Mara. Her name was Mayana Lucy after Peter's mother. He called her 'His little Lucy'. She died of leukemia when she was 11 and David, Mara's first born died in street fighting when he was about 30. David died just after I was born.

I do not have clear evidence or a death certificate, but it appears Henri probably died 3 years ago in the burned-out motorhome. Grandad heard through Mara who was indicated as NOK. Later, the news came through Karol from Mom in a letter.

"Peter and Naomi were to be married when Peter finished his Term of Service. However, in the meantime his father arranged for Peter's marriage to cover his own sin of the flesh."

"Okay, so now meet Peter II who, by the way, is Henri's child by rape of Naomi's only child. Peter II and I were good Buds and had a lot of fun researching. Peter is a University Prof about 9 years my senior. You will meet him one day when they come to Canada to visit."

Jack caught that and teasingly said "Oh so you are maybe thinking of keeping me in the loop eh!" We both had a good laugh, knowing that it was a deep possibility now that we were revealed to each other.

"Back to the Naming" I said "As I was saying, Peter Senior took Peter and I to his office one day and began to give us a history lesson. He suggested I have a DNA evaluation done. Fortunately, that day I could simply whip it out of my backpack as Peter and I had already done so. Without even reading it, Grandad pulled an envelop from his desk. It was addressed to 'Jamie Gillette Parker'. But grandad assured me that was me."

"So, when I got to the Cabin and received the letter from the Lawyer asking me to change my name so he could complete the documentation for the Land Ownership, why would I not become Jamie Gillette Parker? By that time, my Relatives were calling me Jamie already. I like the sound of Jamie. It resonates with who I am. And this Ring I wear was in the package – a Gift from my birth father. I'll find the letter and let you read it in the morning for yourself. It was very touching at the time."

"Come to think of it, 'Jack and Jamie' sound even better than 'Petri and Petra'. Do you agree?"

"Jamie you are my Forever Friend. I do not know how Peter came about. Though I have a strong feeling now. You do not have to tell me until you are ready. We will see how our stories match."

"However, I love that Boy like my own soul. If it helps, the first day we met, he wrapped my heart around his. I felt like I was looking into my own mirror when I was young and wanted to be 'whiter' like my classmates.

And then I met you in high school, whom also had Color. You who set my heart on fire and won my heart those several years back. Though I did not know that the day I first came here to size up the project."

"The only thing I can say for myself is that at that stage in life, the Studious Personality, I was still ADULTerated by my parent's desire that *I Become Somebody*. So, I was so wrapped up in Academia to 'Study *and Becoming Somebody*' that I missed the greatest opportunity in a lifetime. I missed keeping in touch and maybe saving you from trauma."

"Oh, please do not feel sorry for me Jack. Peter is probably my Best Teacher. I would not have him if life were a Dream as we used to visualize it as, and the nightmare hour had not happened."

"Just as Maria grew out of tragedy into an amazing mother of Peter II, I have grown out of the conception of Peter III. We would not have met again; nor would I have what I have, had it not been for the trauma the gardener laid upon me. A lot of my Coaching Clients have a similar story. I understand them on a deep level because of the experiences of my own life."

Jack took a deep searching breath before he opened yet another surprise. "Petra (sorry, I will likely make that mistake a thousand times in the future) Jamie I am Peter's uncle." Tears rolled down his cheeks.

"Peter is my brother's child."

Shocked! I could hardly take it in.

"If you remember I was here to line up this Project. A few days later I was called to appear in court. I simply told you I was called away on a family matter. Yes, I am grateful that you obliged me with waiting it out and providence gave me the opportunity to continue this project even though I had to delay you for a few months."

"The reason for the summons being, I was to identify my brother, whom I had never met. I was in the Legalities of India, South Africa and back to Georgia where he was being charged and eventually sentenced to 'death row.'"

Things began to click in my memory. Things I thought I had left behind. I know Jack recognized that he was causing distress for me, but we both recognized that I needed to know the story to complete my own journey through it. So, I listened.

"And yes, Jamie I saw the camera footage of the evidence your Grandad had to convict him. And yes, though I did not visit with Mara, I saw her countenance and recognized her scorn across the courtroom."

"Though I did not know I was getting to know your Grandad Peter, I did recognize the Bokamosa name as being like yours. I did wonder if it might be related to Henri. No, I did not recognize the woman on the bed or in the bathroom when they showed some of Rami's own footage. That was traumatic enough for a man looking for a Virgin Wife."

"It was not until Peter's birthday and I met your grandad Peter that it all clicked together for me. And to think that I actually saw your trauma unaware. I went home from that birthday with a lot of emotional devastation to work through. It has taken me this time to work through my own emotions, Jamie, to allow this weekend to happen."

"You can still throw me over the bank if you wish." Jack said in half a whisper. I reached for his hand as now it was, he who needed assurance and acceptance <u>FOR WHO HE WAS</u>. I did not hold him responsible for his brother's error.

"Mara would have been Henri's birthmother." I added.

"Unfortunately, my brother, Rami Raju, was not a good man. There were at least 7 in his lineup. Not all were as fortunate as you were. Some are in eternity."

"Your grandad Peter did an excellent job of exposing details that could finally pin him down – a man hunt, on three continents. Grandad Peter told me he did all he could to save you from the traumas of going to court."

"Well actually, Rami probably Hung himself with making the face into the security camera he thought was shut off. Because of that footage, they did not include you in the proceedings, Jamie – evidence enough. Peter Bokamosa did his best to protect you from further traumatization over the matter, especially when it went on for so many years."

"Something else that hung him, was his own laptop. Obviously, he was extremely familiar with security technology. The court in SA exposed his own footage of the camera's he had some how rigged in the Bokamosa Estate House. A recording over of his own voice as he watched his own footage more than once. He was particularly good with security devices. He had not thought that his footage of so many places and activities he had on that little laptop would convict him of more than what you know."

"Jack that is revealing to me. When I hid in the bathroom and could not get myself to feel clean after it happened, and I know this is a part of most of my clients experience too, I could hear his hideous laughter. I wanted to punch through the wall and kill the guy just to shut him up. I could not have imagined that he was watching my frustration. Ouch!"

"It does help me understand my Client's stories even better knowing all this from my own. As hard as this conversation is on you Jack, I can honestly say that all I can feel is pity, as if it is someone else's story. I have done a lot of emotional work to right my perspective and attitude toward bad events. I am not saying bad people, because I know that "It is either LOVE or a Call for LOVE" as we learned years ago in ACIM."

"You know Petri – see there I go too! Anyway, I am so grateful that I had you to study ACIM with in high school. I do not know how often I have thanked my Creator for the techniques I have learned that helped me through the situations and traumas of life. And perhaps the biggest being rejection from parents.

"And part of that training was your kindness Grad Weekend in showing me that I could be with a man who respected my boundaries, my privacy and gave me confidence in my own choices."

"This may sound strange to you Dear Jack, but I am glad this is coming out into the open with you. Obviously, you know more about my 'Missing Years' than I know about yours. What this is doing for me is filling in some gaps or missing pieces that sometimes haunt me, though I can honestly say that this is not stirring trauma nerves. Instead, it is enlightening and reassuring that people can work through troubling time to regain the deep LOVE we were created to be."

"Keep talking Jack, not that I require knowing the rest of the events of your journey at that time, but I do know it will release the trauma of knowing a brother as a criminal."

"Something else I could add is that Naomi told me early in pregnancy that I could let go of the trauma perspective of Peter's conception and give him a more positive conception." I had to giggle before I told him the rest. "I chose us Grad Weekend as if in the gentle touching, we had gone far enough to conceive him."

"Of course, you know we did not, and I respect you for respecting me. And we both know that Peter would have had an exceptionally long gestation period." We both laughed now. It released the tension this conversation had built up to.

"What can we say more? The Creator LOVES us and has kept us until this day." We were still in each other's arms for a long time that evening

Chapter 22

Willow's Wisdom

In the beginning Created – Male & Female created simultaneously and of equal value. Genesis 1:27

– if I believe otherwise, I am believing my Creator forgot the Reason everything was created for, The Procreation of LOVE.

A People that CHOOSES to LOVE as Creation LOVES.

The belief of Genesis 2:18 on to the end of the chapter, undermines my confidence in an All Knowing All LOVING Power I can trust in for my wellbeing.

I would be believing 'The Great Creative Spirit forgot something in The Plan of Creation.'

Forgot the requirement for a Procreative Partner, the Feminine for the Masculine to replicate the LOVE that Creation Is.

Now this is just my take. You can think as you do and that is fine with me. My wonder is if those verses were added when the Holy Scripture of Christian Belief was revised by governing authorities to indoctrinate more firmly Male Dominance.

But as I said, it does not make sense to me to think the Creator missed anything of value in the Plan.

I reviewed some of Deepak's lessons last night. "The end of the masculine force waves and into the feminine power time."

Is this the Final Act in the Masculine War & Force Games? The lesson was recorded at least 2 years before the Scandemic of Fear.

Satan's final kick to survive when the end of evil is at hand.

It is approximately 100 years since Women began to be considered a Person and got the Okay to Vote. It was a good reminder for me as I knew in 2012 that though there were evil days ahead, we were coming into a time where LOVE would Reign and a Back to Eden would happen as Feminine Power became stronger and offered the LOVE.

And yes, as a Native American, before white man forced their ways and beliefs upon us, Our People respected our connection to the Great Spirit as well as to the Energy of All Things.

The sand, the trees, the waters, the animals etc. were all just as important as one another. We all served in our place to provide for the whole Tribe and for the Earth as our Friend and Provider. It is said that we moved to where food was when we exhausted it in the place we were.

That is how white man wrote it. The Reality is that we moved before we damaged the area so that it could regenerate itself. The Great Spirit guided us and told us when it was time to move to another area. The Great Spirit also guided us where to go.

Our long-braided hair was like a warning system to us. No one could sneak up on us from behind without us sensing it. Maybe even among other nationalities, that is why women with long hair sense and feel things that men do not. They sense the LOVE that Created them and their loved ones. They sense what it is to nurture and keep nurturing others and our Earth Mother.

Perhaps it is why Ben is such a good Doctor – he has an excellent balance of both Masculine and Feminine Energy. He senses the requirements of his patience and honors the Knowing that many other Doctors may miss.

Since Jamie moved to the Cove, Ben has been a regular at my home. He has taught me a lot of the Science behind the Knowing of our People. Not that we require Scientific Proof, as often it is flawed in what it has not considered as a part of the whole. But still, it is beneficial when communicating with someone else's *'Educated Mind'*.

There is much written about our warrior nature and survival of the fittest. We were FIT until white man brought their sickness issues to us. We ate from an uncontaminated land. The Great Spirit told us what we could and could not eat to give us Life, to help our women in child birthing pain, to fix wounds that may have happened in The Hunt and many other things.

You see many photos of toothless ancestors. Our ancestors had strong teeth and did not loose them until they began to crave white man's dainties and fluids. The pictures you see are taken or painted after these things began to deteriorate our People.

Please understand, that bringing this information up now is not Against White Man or anything else that happened in history. It is simply to help the reader to understand that our People in their Element are not drunkards, killers, and molesters anymore than the derailed of any nationality.

This document is not against anyone. This is simply to show that in our Element, we were Peaceful. We were The Teachers of the Land; had you cared to listen and hear.

It was White Man's greed for Furs and all things they could take back to show off to their people on another continent that raped the native Americas. Still, it is greed, whether for place, space or face that has us living in a chemical environment that is not sustainable.

Again, it will be the Women (the feminine energy of LOVE) that will Balance the Earth and restore the Harmony of Life between The Great Spirit, all species, plants, and animals.

Whether you are male or female or confused about your gender; look to the Great Spirit once again and ask the Creator to correct the imbalance of masculine and feminine energy.

When deep in our Being we take the responsibility for what is, and feel the Healing of the Nations through our LOVE; only then will the Healing come, and the Sun Shine upon us once again. Not just upon ourselves, but upon all our partners in and on the Earth, the stars and all that places us in the Harmony of LOVE the Creator planned.

So please remember that we were not a War mentality. Warriors as modern man understands warrior is a modern word that was not in our vocabulary.

Yes, we had and still have Braves and Brave Celebrations. A Brave did not go out to bring back skelping or foreskins to show he was brave. Those were practices taught us by the War like natures of those who invaded our peaceful lands. Those nations had to send back to their Leaders the evidence of the battle.

Our Brave Celebration was about the young man being a Good Provider. He showed he was of Age when he could go out by himself in a dark night and then brought back Food for the whole Tribe. The night he was sent out or chose to go, an Elder would follow a distance behind to protect him should adversity arise. The Brave was unaware of this help. It was a secret held by the Elders.

Seldom were we sick as white man calls sickness. What we ate and how we lived gave us wellness, nurtured on the goodness of the land that white man thought we worshipped and apparently it was not their understanding to honor all things living and all things that brought Life.

We honor the Great Spirit that Created all things. We honored the Great Spirit more highly than anything else because the Great Spirit Guided us and gave us sustenance. We sang praises in our lilting way to the Great Spirit and all that is Created for our use to keep life in the Flow of All Life.

It will be when that LOVE for the Great Spirit returns that the Creator's LOVE will return the Flow of All Life. Honor the Creator and Spirit and honor will return to the Earth to give Abundance for every member of our vast family of nature – an Everlasting Promised Land.

Yes, you call the Great Spirit 'God' which is fine with me. However, I have not heard anyone using the Great Spirit or Creator in bad language as your people have taught my people to use your word.

Your word 'God' comes from Greek Mythology. My Great Spirit is not myth. My Great Spirit that Created all things is as Real as the Creation. The LOVE the Great Spirit shares with us is the only Truth there is – LOVE.

Therefore, I am asking all of humanity to examine your beliefs. Do your Beliefs and the actions that show what it is you Believe Honor Creation's Creator?

Honor the Great Creator Spirit? Honor your fellow creations?

Honor the LOVE that you are so you can honor All things living with the LOVE that flows out of you?

When our LOVE is Reigning Above the dark cloud of greed and prejudice; when our LOVE is coming from the Eternal Source of LOVE: then can we see Harmony and Peace on Earth.

Ask with Feeling as if it is already done. Ask for the Healing LOVE that we read of Jesus bringing to the Earth millennia ago.

We all require the prayer:

I am sorry.
Please Forgive me.
Thank You.
I LOVE You.

Chapter 23

And now above the LADDER that rose out of the Chaotic Storm of Insanity – the illusion called *self-will and 'I can do it my way' attitude, the hiding in our fears:* The Resting Place is ours as our vulnerability becomes the Street of Transparent Gold. We are ONE again with the Creator of the Universe – with THE LOVE!

All Eternal Lights glow brighter in gratitude for restoration. All angels offer loving support to keep away darkened thought of former things. Our footprints lighter still upon the Earth keep the LIGHT where it has entered in.

Where we walk Forgiveness gladly goes with us, released in Freedom to Live the NOWING of each moment from a Higher Source of LOVE from within to without.

There is not a Tower, but a Ladder. I saw it very clearly in a Vision one morning. I was inquiring about Belief – What Lord should I be believing and what is simply the *Window Dressing*?

How can I cope with this time of scandemic and harassment?

The Answer - **Rise Above to Reign with Me in the Air**.

Then I saw a Ladder – at the bottom was the pollution and dust of vehicles, people, chemicals and more all in a Dark Cloud of filthy smoggy dust of confusion. There were about 3 faintly visible steps on the Ladder. On each step there was a Word.

The Ladder was narrow at the bottom upon which is written Repent/Change.

The 1st Step reads – Courage.
The 2nd Step reads – Mercy/Forgiveness.
The 3rd Step reads – Trust.
The 4th Step reads – Surrender.
The 5th as we said above is Gold Plaited LOVE
Step 6 is Peaceful.
Step 7 is Harmony or At One – Atonement.

Above the 4th the head is into the Light and reaching for the 5th where LOVE is printed in Shiny Gold. At this point I recognized that the Ladder was completely supported by the LOVE that Created.

Once past 5, the Ladder starts to vanish, and One becomes completely engulfed in the Immensity of the All-Creative LOVE and LIGHT as the only voice (not noise) is a Beautiful Song of Praise.

LOVE – We were created by Eternal LOVE, to BE LOVE, to BE LOVEABLE, to be LOVE Able. We either move further into LOVE or we move away from LOVE.

LOVE is the only Truth.

When I move into that LOVE more fully as I transition into the Life Beyond, I move into the LOVE of the continuous Praise.

If I have not learned to LOVE and Praise in this life, the LOVE Beyond will strangely feel like a hell. I have not experienced it previously and I will not feel comfortable in it.

Yes, my Jesus is the express amplification of the Eternal LOVE for me to learn from and live by. To see what this LOVE resonates like in a human being.

The more LOVE I manifest in this life in living before and to others, the more the LOVE of Jesus is displayed for the world to believe in.

The Holy Spirit, The Great Spirit is the Guiding Spirit that leads me to LOVE as the Eternal LOVES.

I can know a lot of history and knowledge about how things work or do not work and yet not know LOVE. LOVE as an untainted child loves and that is all I really need to know.

Serve the Creator of LOVE with All my Heart; with All my Soul; with All my Strength and with all my mind. Intellectual mind/ ego mind may be a good tool but not a profitable ruler.

From this, LOVE my neighbour as myself.

If my LOVE of the Being I am created to BE is of poor quality, that will be the quality of Love going out of my life to others.

If I LOVE with my Creator's LOVE from within to without, there is complete confidence to LOVE as I was created to LOVE.

So, perhaps Self LOVE is what I am all about to teach others the necessity of LOVE from within to flow out.

Chapter 24

Monday morning Jack called in to work and got everybody going. He also called Willow and asked if she was open to keeping Peter for another overnight. There were a few things he wanted to communicate with Jamie about.

Willow was more than happy to do so. She called me to reassure me that Peter and she had a project they must finish before he came home. Tomorrow they would come about 5 and bring the evening meal with them.

About 10, Jack came over and sat down on the deck. He knew I had a morning Client Call, and I would be down when I finished.

The rest of the day was mine to reflect and relax. Why I did not even have to make a meal if I did not wish to. But then.........

Jack would soon be leaving. I required a Goodbye hug before he left. I ran down the stairs and was surprised by his presence on the deck below. He was gazing out across the cove. He had a letter and a few other papers in his lap. It did not look like he was preparing to leave very soon.

"Morning Sir! Did you sleep well?" I asked.

"Excellent Dear Jamie! I am inclined to claim that Cabin. What is the yearly rent for it?" he smiled.

I gave him a quizzical look. "Are you serious? I never thought about folks wanting to rent indefinitely." And I sat down beside him. "Anyway, Dear Jack, you know I would never consider a rental to you. I believe we are Family. I am a lover of Guests."

Jack said "I called in to work, and everyone knows what they are to do this week. I think I could do with a week off. After finding this:" he raised the handful of papers, "I decided to stay a few more days. I will do my best to lie low and not interfere with your normal week."

"I brought a box of papers that belonged to my parents. Most of their stuff has been in storage. I have not looked through, if you can believe it. I decided to bring a box with me and sort through this weekend."

"Well, I dug into it last night when sleep was the last thing my busy mind wanted to do. I found some interesting information I am trying to digest and make sense of."

"Maybe I require the assistance of a Lifestyle Designer. Or at least a Life Coach."

"Then maybe we require Willow's assistance" I offered.

"Right! But I expect we can understand it, as it is in plain English. No legal jargon here, but a little ruffling for me."

Jack gave me three sheets of paper that were stapled together.

I began to scan them. The first page was a birth registration that stated Place of Birth as 'Home' and the address of where he grew up.

The second was a letter written by his mother.

Dear Petri,

I will be dead and gone by the time you find these documents.

This may come as a surprise to you. We never had the heart to tell you upfront. Our hearts were saddened at the time to know that Rami had left someone so young in this state after his home visit his first year of University.

For whatever reason, he did not come home again. We lost track of him after your birth. Why? We may never know.

Petri, I was awakened early one May day to the tiny cry of a baby. The doorbell had rung earlier, but being sleepy, I saw no reason to rush to it until morning light. Then the cry was heard again, and louder this time.

When I went to the door, there you were in a box wrapped in a towel. There was a handwritten note that you will find attached.

Because we knew you were only a few hours old, and the note claimed you to be Rami's child, we simply registered you as our own, not wanting to take our own son to law. Who would even know?

The third was a note from a young girl. She claimed she was 13 and the mother of Rami's child. She could not keep the child because she desired to finish her education. She claimed her family did not know about the birth since she had been kicked out of home a few months before he was born. She claimed no one else knew, as she had delivered the baby herself; but could not look after any medical expenses.

"Who is she?" Jack asked. "This is my MOTHER!"

"My GRANDPARENTS had heart and raised me apparently Jamie."

"I have no idea. I have no idea how she could be found either. That is young to be on your own. But then Sara was not much older when she chose the Street Life. And Mara conceived David when she was about that age. Oh my!"

We both sat there rather stunned for several minutes. I stood up and walked to the rail, looking out across the Cove gathering what I could from the InnerNet.

Is there any calming wisdom I could add to Jack's revelation? He would have grown with a different set of beliefs and challenges had this been revealed to him as a child. Perhaps he is lucky that his parentage revelation arrived at an age he could process it in a mature manner. How strange life can be!

I was even more thankful for the revelation coming at this point for him. He may not be the Jack I know and love now, if he would have had this knowledge when he was a child.

I heard Jack come across the deck and turned to face him.

We both drew the conclusion simultaneously. "Jack, you are not only Peter's uncle. You are Peter's half-brother as well."

He gathered me into his arms.

"Yes, Jamie!" and we stood together for several minutes in silence, heartbeat to heartbeat. How strange life can be!

Eventually Jack broke the silence.

"Jamie? May I have the privilege of being Peter's step-father as well – Dad to my own little brother?"

Epilogue

This Novel began to Download on September 27. This final chapter was downloaded on January 27. I had no idea how this Book would end. As I told you in the beginning 'You may know because you hold a completed Book. I did not.'

For anyone, for everyone, you have a Book within you. Write. Even if it is only for your own healing emotionally. It is well worth it and a valuable Emotional Cleansing.

I am a different woman today for having written this book.

Yes, 20 years ago when I began to compile the materials and write, I would never have written this Novel. Even a year ago, when it became evident that I must write about sexual trauma, I resisted. Perhaps that is when the STOP TO WILL power stopped and I had nowhere to go in writing.

September brought Curiosity.

Without that Curiosity, that letting go of my own thoughts of what to include, the letting go of EGO, followed by surrender and transparency, to become vulnerable and to simply download; you would not be holding this Book.

Enjoy!

Gift your friends and family. You will know who would benefit from having their own copy. With every copy sold, there is a Frolic Book to download and play in.

And now watch for the Sequel:

"You've Got a Hair Out of Place

— The Family Wedding"

Reading List

1. A Course In Miracles combined volume – Foundation for Inner Peace. www.acim.org
2. The Holy Bible
3. Power vs. Force – The Hidden Determinants of Human Behavior
4. The Eye of the I – From which Nothing is Hidden
   a. David R. Hawkins, M.D., Ph.D.

5. Heal Your Life – Louise L. Hay
6. Healing Oils of the Bible – Dr. David Stewart
7. My favorite fiction author – Nicholas Sparks
8. Ho'oponopono and Dr. Joe Vitale with whom I was introduced to the Hawaiian Prayer.
9. Christy Whitman with whom I took Quantum Success Coaching.
10. Too numerous are all the authors and course presenters to list here. If you notice a thread of your work, I honor your giving me a Lifelong Project.
11. Above all I Honor the All-Creative Source of LOVE that taught me to "Seek the Kingdom of LOVE" first and all things would be added. Just maybe that is the source from which this Book is downloaded.

About the Author

Canadian born. Challenged by sexual abuse, brain compromise due to vehicle accidents, and over medicated as a child and young woman.

Challenges led to Research as to what keeps us in Wellness, and what interrupts wellness.

At age 33 told that within 10 years she would be sentenced to a wheelchair – 7 major diagnosis including MS, Manic Depression, Lupus, Pre-Diabetic and Osteoporosis etc.

She is the mother of 3 grown Children, 5 Grandchildren and a Host of Friends and Clients that keep her on her toes with learning and staying abreast of modern technology, wellness wisdom and emotional harmony.

A **Lifestyle Designer** for more than 30 years.

An Emotional Empowerment Coach since 2001.

Married to the 1st Husband for over 50 years.

CPSIA information can be obtained
at www.ICGtesting.com
Printed in the USA
BVHW030547020621
608589BV00001B/2